STOP for the ONE

RAVI KAPOOR

Foreword by Carol Mohan

STOP FOR THE ONE

Copyright © 2024 Ravi Kapoor

Contact Ravi Kapoor: gripofgrace309@gmail.com

All rights reserved. No part of this publication may be reproduced, stored in a retrieval system, or transmitted in any form by means of electronic, mechanical, photocopying, recording, or otherwise, except for the inclusion of brief quotations in a review, without prior permission in writing from the author and publisher.

Edited by Gwen Denlinger Cox

Cover Design by Pastor J. Winters

Book Layout by Shannon Crowley, Treasure Image & Publishing—TreasureImagePublishing.com

DEDICATION

This book would not have been possible without the inspiration and encouragement of one special person in my life.

Dear Renu was more than my sister, she was my constant companion, treasured friend and confidant. She was like a caring mother, and was also a partner in ministry. No words can fully express what my dear sister Renu meant to me. Such a gift from God!!!

We shared life together in one way or another every day. We confided in each other and walked closely through all of life's ups and downs. Valleys were made easier and mountain tops more full of joy, when we were together.

Renu dearly loved the Lord and was wholly devoted to Him. God was very real to her. She was a rare kind of person who never kept any hurt, bitterness, hatred, or anger towards anyone. She was at peace with God and always lived in peace with everyone.

If someone had something against her, even if it was not her fault, she would humble herself and go to that person to ask for forgiveness and make peace.

Renu always took a strong stand for her faith and loved to share about the love of Jesus with others.

When we were together, I often noticed that she had a silent elegance about her. She did not speak much, but her graceful presence spoke volumes and was a quiet inspiration to those around her. She was a unique soul to be such a blessing without saying a word. She gloriously radiated our Lord's love, and those around her could sense it.

She was always there for me. We traveled out of Bangalore on different occasions to a quiet place so I could spend much time with the Lord in prayer and concentrate on writing. She was able to discern when I needed time alone and when I needed her sweet presence to refresh me and help me relax. She was a gentle encouragement and quiet source of strength to me as we spent so much time together in fellowship, prayer, and worshiping our beloved Jesus.

She always came to my home to care for me when I wasn't feeling well, then stayed a few extra days so I wouldn't have to be alone. She was an excellent cook and delighted to feed me delicious food, with her characteristic nonstop love.

Dear sister Renu was promoted to being in the presence

of her beloved Jesus in Heaven on 30th December, 2020. She has left an impact on me and all who knew her in this life. I will forever be thankful to God for her influence in my life, her unending support, unconditional love, enduring patience and deep understanding.

This book has come to fruition by God's grace and many, many prayers of dear Renu. I pray it will touch all who read it with the love and grace of God that was expressed through the life of my beloved sister Renu.

STOP FOR THE ONE

ACKNOWLEDGEMENTS

Before all else, I want to thank God for His goodness to me and for helping me to put into words what is on my heart. All glory goes to Him alone.

This book could have never been completed without the help and prayers of so many friends both near and far, who encouraged me every step of the way, and cheered my progress. I am blessed by your love and faithfulness.

I would specifically like to thank:

Linda Valen: Thank you for being an inspiration! God used your words ten years ago to encourage me to write a book. I still have the message you wrote to me, which surprised me and gave me the courage to pursue becoming an author!

You said, "Have you ever thought of writing a book? You have a real gift with words but you also communicate so deeply with your heart by the words you choose. You have a GIFT of telling stories (testimonies)!"

Thank you for standing with me, believing in me, and giving me the first push that I needed. I highly appreciate you! Thank you for taking time out of an extremely busy schedule to read through my manuscript, give advice when needed, and do the final proofreading.

Gwen Denlinger Cox: Just wanted to express my deep gratitude for offering your valuable time and skills to edit each chapter and make sure what was in my heart came across clearly. Thank you so much for your support. This book would have not been possible without your tremendous contribution. You are truly a gift from God.

Ray Horton: Thank you for investing so much of your time to proofread and offer valuable suggestions. Words cannot express how deeply I appreciate your support and encouragement. You are a blessing!

Pastor J. Winters: I want to convey my heartfelt thanks to you for your contribution in designing the cover. You agreed to help me immediately when I asked, and your desire to assist me touched my heart deeply. It is excellently done and very appealing in its arrangement. I am most grateful!

Tarun Das: God has blessed you with so many talents, one of them being the gift of photography. Thank you for my picture.

Shannon Cowley: Thank you for publishing my book, the finished product of a dream that began a long time ago.

ENDORSEMENTS

Stop for the One is the perfect sequel to Brother Ravi's first book, Lost and Found. His first book being the testimony of his salvation and how God moved in his early ministry captivates your heart.

This book shares the lifestyle God has called him to live. This is a ministry calling on his life but so much more. Ministries can come and go or even evolve from one area to another, but a lifestyle is who you are in every area of your life.

It is your identity in Christ, who you are when everyone is looking and when no one is there to see. What Brother Ravi shares with us in this, his second book, one of many to come I pray, is a lifestyle of being Jesus to "the one" God brings along our pathway each day.

I found the experiences of his life shared in these pages to be not only inspiring but motivating. It has caused me to not only open my eyes to "the one" but to be looking for "the one." He shows us how God orchestrates the simple events of our everyday lives to connect us with those who desperately need God. We are His hands and feet, His mouth and heart for those in need of His love.

However, this is not just a book of Brother Ravi's experiences in life. There are words of God's Wisdom and instruction as well. I found myself taking notes to look back on later. Things I am praying for Holy Spirit to make a part of who I am!

There is no doubt that Brother Ravi has a deep love for God that has come through an intimate relationship with Jesus! That love for God and from God flows across every page. It draws me in and creates within my heart a desire for this deeper intimate relationship with my Jesus. Read and enjoy, knowing that as you do, God will touch your heart with His love and compassion for "the one"!

In Matthew 18:10-14, Jesus tells the parable of the lost sheep to show us just how important "the one" is to His heart. He would leave the 99 to seek the 1 lost sheep. May we all be like Jesus and become, as Brother Ravi, a servant of God to, "*Stop for the One*"!

SHARON JOYLEA DAVIS

Ravi is God's love letter to all he encounters. Someone once said, "The world does not read it's Bible but it reads it's Christians." Ravi is a good read, a man full of the tenderness of God toward the lost, the last, the little, and the lame. You will love his stories.

FAWN PARISH
People Developer, Author/Speaker
International Reconciliation Coalition

Endorsements

What does the genuine love of Jesus look like in this world? You will find out as you read Ravi Kapoor's book, *Stop for the One*. Ravi can write a book like this because he lives a lifestyle of stopping for those who are hurting!

His stories of the leadings of Holy Spirit to the many he encounters will captivate and challenge you to a new level of living for Jesus and reaching out to others!

Because of the brokenness Ravi experienced before falling radically in love with Jesus, he walks in an anointing of listening love, sincere compassion and life-giving actions that are transforming the lonely, lost, broken, hopeless, addicted, suicidal people he meets and brings them to Jesus. You will never be the same after you read these true testimonies.

LINDA VALEN
Ministry Director, Master Potter, Inc.
jillaustinlegacy.com

"*Stop for the One*" is a powerful, convicting flood of intriguing testimony of one man, who through the love of Christ, daily reaches out to and transforms through Christ the lives of so many hurting people in India.

Truly, Ravi Kapoor is a living testimony of the fulfillment of Paul's exhortation to the church in Galatia to "Bear one another's burdens, and so fulfill the law of Christ." Having the heart of a true shepherd, Ravi fulfills the ministry of an evangelist as he compassionately ministers the love of Christ to so many.

I highly recommend *"Stop for the One"* to anyone who is serious about becoming a living "epistle known and read of all men" for the cause of Jesus Christ.

ROBERT J. WINTERS, DMIN
Senior Pastor, Prepare the Way International Church
Phoenix, AZ, U.S.A.

Over the years, I have heard people give testimony of the importance of sharing God's love with just one soul. Often these stories end by revealing the familiar name of a famous person who won large numbers of people to Christ: Billy Graham, Oral Roberts are examples. But what about the one God saves who just like you and me seldom reaches fame and glory? Is that person's story worth telling? Yes, it is!

Ravi Kapoor tells of his encounters with the everyday person who is singled out by God to receive love, healing and salvation. This book stresses that God is everywhere active in the affairs of the hurting and hopeless and has servants available to rescue the lost and dying. It is a beautiful story of how powerful everyday encounters can be when we are led by God to be His voice, hands and feet. You will enjoy every page that you read just as I did.

REV. BARBARA WILLIAMS
President and Founder, The Ministry of the Watchman, Intl.
ministryofthewatchman.com

Endorsements

If your heart has been touched by The Holy Spirit of God with a tear, a tug, a prayer, a lump in your throat for the hurting, the lonely, the ravaged, the abused and lost ones, then this book "*Stop for the One*" is a must.

The author has that kind of heart given to him by God, and as you read about some of the encounters that the Spirit has brought him to, I pray you will receive an impartation of God's Love for "The One" just as Ravi Kapoor has.

BARBARA MANNING
Lover of God
Lover of The Hurting

Get ready for your heart to be filled, and overflow with so much love and compassion when you read the pages of this book! Not only is this book full of love, but it teaches us what true sacrifice and humility is really all about.

I invite you to walk along with the author, line upon line, and experience the awesome love of God as he encounters each divine appointment. We should all desire to be used by God in this way, which displays God's deep abiding love for mankind. To God be the glory!

REV. SHIRLEY CAMP
Author, *The Prize: The High Calling and The Great Commission*
The Ministry of the Watchman, Intl.
ministryofthewatchman.com

In the many years that I have known Ravi Kapoor, I have found him consistently to be like Barnabas, "The Son of Encouragement." Many times, when I have struggled with discouragement, I have found an unsolicited word of comfort and edification from him in my email or in a private message. By the Spirit of God, he takes action to reach out to others. I believe Ravi lives his daily life with a single goal to praise Jesus and glorify the Father. He does this well.

This book chronicles some special moments in his life where he has especially seen God's hands and feet working through his. You will be encouraged to read it.

REV. JUDY A BAUMAN
International Speaker
Founder, The Father's Love Int'l Ministries
Author, **Jewels from the River, Jewels from the Harvest,**
and **Jewels from Judy**

If you have been searching for a person who—like Jesus—is love in the flesh, love in action, then you need look no further. In the pages of Ravi's book you will find a man who is passionately in love with Jesus. His single minded purpose in life beside worshiping God and getting to know and obey Him, is to pour out his life and his love on those whose lives have become defined by loss, pain, grief, despair, deprivation, and hopelessness.

The hallmark of his evangelistic approach is expressing a sacred sensitivity to the one who is to be the recipient of his love and attention. Ravi's words, his testimonies of the broken people who God has brought to him will doubtless inspire you, as they have me.

He, like Jesus, loves people out of their pain and distress in tangible ways. He gets people to Jesus by loving them in a hands on, selfless, practical, time consuming, manner. This life style of loving service to the needy and broken hearted will become magnetic as you read about the many lives that have been set free because Ravi was led to 'Stop for the One'.

SANDRA WEAVER
A Lover of Jesus

Ravi is a great man of God, sold out and surrendered to the Lord and ministering to those hurting and broken. I highly encourage you to read this book. He will challenge you to 'get out of the box'-to take God's Word as truth-instruction and literally living like Jesus. Laying aside your plans and allowing God to take your hand and lead you on an amazing journey. There is NO limit to what God can do through you, if you are willing to listen and be obedient. As you read this book and allow the Holy Spirit to set a holy fire burning deep within and bring a Luke 4:18 anointing to set the captives free, recover the sight of the blind and bring hope to the downtrodden and hopeless!

PATTY MERRITT
Oklahoma, USA Prayer Ministry Pastor

I have known Ravi Kapoor for a number of years.

I know of few if any who say they love the Lord who have done more in the way of serving so humbly and with so much success that I think only the Lord sees. His experiences are many and I personally know that experiences are what transforms those touched by them but is the Lord's touch on those who deliver them. In a time where many are afraid of tomorrow, Ravi gives hope not only for then but for the future here and the hereafter. His name is already written in the heavens and by reading this book you will get a bit closer yourself.

DENNIS BOOTH
Author, Seer, Missionary.

My prayer partner from halfway around the globe, my dear friend Ravi Kapoor, is addicted to love—love of God and love of people. This is clearly seen in his latest book, *Stop for the One*. And that addiction is transferable, inspiring others to love not just in word but in deed.

When I was baptized in the Holy Spirit nearly 50 years ago, the Lord Jesus' compassion for people suddenly came upon me. I'd walk down the street wondering about each person I saw, wondering what they had gone through, and prayed.

Having been in almost daily contact with brother Ravi for several years, that first love has been reinvigorated in me by his example.

Endorsements

God will do the same for you as you read *Stop for the One*. God has used his example to have more of an impact on my life than most people, even though he lives in far-off India.

Ravi's narratives of personal encounters with hurting people go straight to the heart and inspire us to be more for those God loves in this lost and hurting world around us.

One thing about Ravi, he is authentic, and his life reflects what he writes about. The Lord's unconditional love truly flows through him to others. You too will be impacted as you read the many testimonies of the workings of the Lord through this humble man of God.

Several quotes from *Stop for the One* reveal Ravi's heart:

"I pray before every word I speak and move I make."

"I'm careful to follow Spirit's leading taking steps slowly, with much prayer. I don't want to do things my own way"

"To our Lord belongs all the glory; we must NEVER feel entitled to share any of it with Him! I am a mere vessel."

Do you sense the Lord calling you higher? As you read this book of testimonies, may the Lord inspire your own life to be used more by Him.

RAY E HORTON,
Awakening Ministries
Erie, Pennsylvania, USA

Ravi Kapoor is one of the very special people that I have met along the path of life. His care and compassion for those who are hurting is vast. His HUGE heart for those in need, shares the limitless love of Jesus wherever he is and with whomever he is ministering to. Ravi always stands out in this way to me. I know you will greatly enjoy reading this amazing book of just some of his beautiful and touching God journeys.

JOHN TUSSEY
Pianist, Composer
johntussey.com

TABLE OF CONTENTS

DEDICATION 3

ACKNOWLEDGEMENTS 7

ENDORSEMENTS 9

FOREWORD 21

INTRODUCTION 27

CHAPTER ONE... 33
   Rainbow in the Sky

CHAPTER TWO... 41
   Compassionate Caring

CHAPTER THREE.. 51
   A Night Out with God

CHAPTER FOUR.. 59
   Set Free From the Chains That Bound Me

CHAPTER FIVE 79
   Search Hard to Bless Someone!

CHAPTER SIX 85
   When the Lord Told Me to Take a Left Turn

CHAPTER SEVEN.. 95
   The Healing Power of Listening

CHAPTER EIGHT 109
   The Compelling Power of Love!

CHAPTER NINE 131
   He Saw a Different Kind of Love

CHAPTER TEN 153
   A Love That Shatters Addictions

CHAPTER ELEVEN 177
   Love, off the Clock

CHAPTER TWELVE 191
   Love STOPS!

CHAPTER THIRTEEN 201
   Love Sees When Others Turn Away

CHAPTER FOURTEEN 213
   Love Pays Attention

CHAPTER FIFTEEN 223
   Moved by Compassion

CHAPTER SIXTEEN 237
   From the Depths of Despair
   to Heights of Joy

CHAPTER SEVENTEEN 271
   Love as a Way of Life

ABOUT THE AUTHOR 293

FOREWORD

I have known Ravi since 2012 where I first "met" him through a Facebook prayer group.

It's amazing how you can be so impacted by someone you have never met in person; but in getting to know Ravi through many messages back and forth and in particular in reading his first book "Lost and Found," and now this book "*Stop for the One*" I have found myself not just knowing Ravi on a deeper level, but being challenged, encouraged and discipled on a deeper level too!

I have been privileged, along with many others, to pray for Ravi and for some of those he has ministered to. He, in turn, has become a trusted, loving brother and friend who I can share anything with and it will remain safely tucked in his heart and only used for prayerful purposes.

Authentic, loving, kind, merciful, humble, available… These are some of the many words I would attribute to Ravi Kapoor. Ravi's life and heart are so consumed by God's love to reach the lost and broken-hearted. His ministry is to the lost, the lonely, the least and the last. Ravi is a rare treasure.

Mother Theresa's quote sums up Ravi beautifully: "I am a little pencil in the hand of a writing God who is sending a love letter to the world."

"*Stop for the One*" is full of deep and beautiful stories of lives transformed by the power of LOVE; the power of LOVE through one man who has found the joy of living for Jesus, listening sensitively to Holy Spirit and allowing God's outrageous love to move in and through him. I was continually struck by the simplicity and humility of Ravi's walk with the Holy Spirit, but also his uncompromising laying down of his life. Although he is just a man, and must choose each time to say "yes" to God and "no" to his own flesh of ease and compromise, he has learnt to yield to the Holy Spirit's direction, knowing that a great adventure of some kind lay ahead.

The reader will be enthralled as they hear of the many God adventures for Ravi with his scooter as He leads him to intense encounters of emotions displayed, behaviours that many Christian believers would shun; yet Ravi keeps saying "yes" to God letting Him do His work in and through Ravi's life bringing that "one" through many days, weeks or even months to a knowledge and dependence upon God Himself.

For each one, Ravi gives all the glory to God as he delights in seeing those he is called to minister to move into their own destiny and purpose for which God has called them.

I love the way Ravi weaves many quotes of others who speak with profound depth; truth-filled gems to strengthen the heartbeat of this book.

Many of the quotations bring us back to a critical truth; for surely we, the reader, need to be reminded of some of these truths again and again before we will really listen and have them planted deep in our hearts, let alone walk in them.

Many of us may be captivated by the divine appointments, the powerful testimonies of changed lives and the work of Father, Son and Holy Spirit through Ravi's ministry; but again and again we see these results simply through a yielded vessel and an incredible laying down of his own life.

Ravi has no desire for "ministry" or "titles," even delaying a pre-planned speaking ministry to stop for that ONE, giving that ONE his entire attention, heart and love.

Another reason for Ravi's intimate and fruitful life in God is that he is very aware of his own calling and ministry that the Lord has given him. He is at ease and free with it; a huge empathy and calling for the lost, lonely, discouraged, depressed, down and out. There is no one or any situation that Ravi would turn away from as the Lord leads him daily to those who need God through him.

There is a challenge to all of us to walk the walk of a truly surrendered Jesus-loving heart; soft, tender, flexible and ready to obey even if it hurts us and especially when we need to step away from our "spiritual agendas and schedules".

The importance of opening up our spiritual eyes so we can see the hearts that are hurting, in pain, in desperate need.

In every story shared and every person ministered to, Ravi continually brings his reader back to the truth that there is only ONE who can love; the God who loves us unconditionally, perfectly, faithfully; the God who is there always, in and through every season of our lives, who will always be the only ONE who will never abandon or leave us alone.

Ravi has a deep sensitivity to the needs of others to be able to love them as they are, where they are; indeed it is the unique love of Jesus for each one. He is always fully present with each one, giving them his full attention.

Ravi has learned to listen, move with and allow the Holy Spirit to lead him in every meeting. He has learned the essential, life-giving skill of listening to the broken one; listening to their cries, their unspoken pain, their silence; and just being with them in that place of pain.

Then, he allows the loving, kind words of the Lord to speak through him. Because of his sensitivity to the Holy Spirit, God's love through Ravi has become an amazing evangelism tool. Ravi IS the walking, talking Bible to those He meets. He allows Jesus to BE in and through Him to those he meets. He is careful to bring people to Jesus and not to himself. He continually guides others to Jesus and does not in any way expect applause, but lives in humility and grace.

Ravi has learned how to walk and work WITH God. He has learned that there is a cost, a laying down of his own life, in order for God's will and purpose to be fully realized in another's life. He lives this life of love.

As you read this book, be ready to be taken on many beautiful journeys, encouraged and challenged to journey more simply and freely with God and to receive more deeply, in your own life, the astounding and transforming love of God.

May you be blessed, graced, strengthened and sent out each day to serve the Lord in the way that He is speaking to you. May you go and *"Stop for the One."*

CAROL MAHON (G.R.S.M LONDON)
Prophetic Minister, Minstrel and Teacher Pastoral Counsellor

STOP FOR THE ONE

INTRODUCTION

To my devoted readers: I pray as you read through each chapter within this book that you will see less of me and more of my Lord and Savior, Jesus Christ. To you, I will reveal my personal step-by-step journey through the way of life God has called all of us to pursue.

The innermost desire of my heart is to follow my Jesus in every way; this is what led me to this lifestyle. The stories that follow can happen to anyone who is sold out for Him and willing to go where He says to go and touch lives, regardless of what others may think! The Bible gives us many examples where Jesus and His disciples lived this out.

In Luke 10:25-37, we find the parable best known as "The Good Samaritan." Most of us have read it personally or heard it told. We can all agree that stopping for someone in need is good. The question we need to ask ourselves is, "Do I practice this in my own life?"

There are times as we move through our busy day, when we feel God nudge us. We know He is guiding and encouraging us to go and do something which will interrupt our carefully laid plans. Often we ignore these promptings because we think we don't have time. Our own plans are more important.

People are waiting on us, depending on us. Doing what God has asked would make us uncomfortable. Maybe we feel it just doesn't make any sense, or that we heard Him wrong. Surely someone else would be better for this task. We can find numerous reasons to ignore what God is asking of us.

We must remember that every act of obedience requires sacrifice. There is that split-second moment when we must decide whether the sacrifice required is one we are willing to make. I pray as you read this book that you will come to feel as I do, for I have seen the fruits of these sacrifices. The results of obedience are worth any inconvenience.

Our obedience to God releases His blessings to flow from Heaven to earth for everyone, including us. We do, however, have a choice and Scripture clearly shows what can happen if we choose not to follow God's leading.

This book is not about ignoring God's voice. It is instead a testimony of what can happen when we choose obedience and see first-hand the portals of heavenly blessing open and flow down here to earth. Many times when these promptings don't make sense to us, it is not until we obey that we see His purposes fully revealed.

These moments of discovery and wonder are part of the great blessings God desires to pour out on the earth. He does this in and through His beloved children, you and I! God's desire is always to bless!

As you read of my personal experiences I am sure you will comprehend that God's intent was not for this to be a random or occasional event that is only for a select few people. He designed this to be a blueprint for all of His children as we go through life. It was in fact taught by Jesus, Himself.

In Matthew 22:36-40, we read of a Pharisee who challenged Jesus with the intent of embarrassing and discrediting Him. Jesus instead laid out in a few words the two main things we must do to please God, "You must love the Lord your God with all your heart, all your soul, and all your mind. This is the first and greatest commandment.

A second is equally important: Love your neighbor as yourself. The entire law and all demands of the prophets are based on these two commandments."

I would like to propose that we can not do either of these two commandments without also doing the other. We must love God before we can truly love others.

How can we sincerely help those who are broken, suffering, downtrodden, or "unlovable," which is what the man in the Good Samaritan parable was thought of by others, if we do not love God? We must also love those we are led to, to demonstrate our love for God!

This is the lifestyle God has called: STOP FOR THE ONE!

Every parable or story Jesus ever told had deep meaning and illustrated an important Kingdom principle for our lives. This one is no exception. We will look at this Scripture later in more detail. For now, I mention it as a perfect example of how we are to *Stop for the One*.

I pray as you read the experiences I have shared, that you will see that the acts of kindness shown to these precious people God brought to me have flowed from a yielded heart full of His love. I can not hold it back!

May the eyes of your heart be opened to see the intense, personal LOVE our Father has for everyone mentioned within these pages. I pray you will also grasp that His passion for YOU is every bit as fervent.

May your life be changed as you read about what just one fully surrendered heart can accomplish, and may you be encouraged to *Stop for the One* the Lord sends your way. There are truly people ONLY YOU can reach and touch with His love.

Will you take the time to reach out and rescue those dear souls from their turmoil and suffering, and point them to Jesus?

STOP FOR THE ONE

CHAPTER ONE

Rainbow in the Sky

The Testimony of a Dear Friend's Daughter

My Mother, Mrs. D. Gnanasugirtham, was beginning to recover after a serious heart attack. She was preparing herself to eventually get back to work at the Telecommunications Department where she had worked before.

Those were very bleak times for our family. We were not able to connect with the ministers we knew at that time so we had to do without the prayers and encouraging messages they would have offered.

Mrs. Hongol was a dear friend of the family. Her only son had met with an accident and was being ministered to by an evangelist. I do not remember the exact date, but one day Mrs. Hongol brought the evangelist to our home.

He had been having problems with his landline and had come to meet my father, Mr. G. Devaraj, who had also worked at the Department of Telecommunications and could possibly help him with his landline problem.

The next time I saw this man was when my maternal aunt, Hilda Auntie, and I were on the terrace. It had just rained, and we saw the evangelist entering our home.

We turned to watch him, then talked with each other and wondered if he really was a man of God. As we turned back around we saw a colorful rainbow in the sky! Taking it to be a sign from the LORD JESUS, we rushed down the stairs and heard the evangelist praying aloud.

Like music from heaven, we could hear the heart of the LORD GOD in his prayer. We could sense the Spirit of God in his prayer and in his voice.

The evangelist became a part of our family. He was a trusted friend to my father and mother, and a brother and uncle to my maternal aunt, my two brothers, and myself.

My mother made sure he was invited for every special event within our home. We shared experiences and meals together and we grew even closer to each other.

Chapter One

Every time my mother or father was admitted to the hospital, the evangelist would visit them, then spend time with the family and pray with us.

One day, my mother's blood pressure went very high. She was home and could not do anything. We tried praying, giving medication, and everything else we could think of, but nothing seemed to work. She refused to see the doctor. I still remember what a difficult day this was! We finally decided to call the evangelist. He rode seven kilometers to come and pray for my mother. Shortly after the prayer, she recovered!

He was a good friend to my father. My father attended the evangelist's prayer meetings where he would intercede for our family and others as well. If my father needed to be somewhere and needed help getting there, the evangelist would personally pick him up, then drop him off where he needed to be.

After completing my Master's degree, I was determined to have a more intimate relationship with God, desiring greatly to know HIM face-to-face.

My favorite portion in the Bible since childhood has been Exodus Chapter 33 to 34, because mortal man got to see the Glory of God.

One day, in the midst of my searching, the evangelist came to our home. While praying for me, he quoted this very portion of Scripture that was my favorite. This confirmation of God's love for me gave me courage then and continues to give me strength now in my pursuit of the LORD GOD OF THE BIBLE.

The evangelist continued to minister to us in troubled times. He kept making it clear that a deep relationship with THE LORD was the most important goal of our walk with GOD. After a heart-to-heart conversation with us, the evangelist would always end every visit to our home with a prayer of intercession for our family.

My mother passed away on the 7th of October 2005. The evangelist was there with us. A few hours before she passed away, he prayed for her in the ICU. Later he told us that she was so intimately connected with the LORD, that it could be plainly seen on her face.

The evangelist was not the only one through whom the LORD GOD worked miracles, signs and wonders. We met many others who also made sure we knew a relationship with the LORD GOD was the most important aspect of following Him, yet for this testimony I shall focus on him and what he did personally for us, on behalf of our LORD.

Chapter One

On the 26th of May 2021, my father successfully underwent a colonoscopy. He had been suffering from a urinary tract infection for a long time, and due to that as well as his age, this procedure was a bit risky. After returning to the ward, we saw a huge rainbow outside. It was large, but the colours were subdued.

Looking back now, it seems like the LORD was telling me, "Okay. You know I can do miracles, and show you signs and wonders, but are you ready to trust Me to do what's best for you and your father? Are you ready to accept My will, no matter what it may be?"

On 24th June 2021, my Father went to be with the LORD. The evangelist prayed for us over the phone every day during my father's stay at the hospital.

Because of the COVID restrictions, he was not able to come and visit my father in person at the hospital, but his prayers gave us strength.

Through all of this, the LORD GOD—the LORD JESUS—used the evangelist to continually remind me that nothing can be a substitute for my relationship with Him. This is what has carried me through all I have been through and continues to sustain me even now.

My past was in God's hands, my present is too. And, I know He is already there in the future. He holds everything all together.

THE LORD GOD continues to use the evangelist, brother Ravi Kapoor, to be available and minister to my family and I, and many others lives in times of both joy and sorrow. The LORD JESUS continues to reiterate through him that a PERSONAL, INTIMATE RELATIONSHIP WITH THE LORD GOD OF THE BIBLE is what we were created to have.

Every time I see a rainbow in the sky, I remember God's promise to our great forefather Noah, but I also see "Relationship with God" written all over it.

At a time when exalted ministers of GOD are celebrated and in the spotlight, it is important to remember the humble servants of GOD who carry the burden of HIS heart and show HIS love to the ones who are in desperate need of it, on the sidelines. It is not just a matter of giving an excellent three point sermon from a pulpit where thousands are watching, but sometimes merely being a friend to just that one person in need. These servants are doing so without demanding attention or underlining that they are ministers of GOD.

Chapter One

Brother Ravi was introduced to my parents by Mrs. Hongol because he had a problem with his telephone, but GOD used this casual meeting to birth the start of a brand new friendship.

This friendship turned into fellowship with a genuine minister for the Lord God—who by example and also through his words caused my family's relationship with God to be strengthened and reach new levels of intimacy with Him.

May all praise, glory, honor, and majesty be ascribed to the LORD OUR GOD, alone. It is He who created us and died and rose again for us.

It is He who now intercedes with THE FATHER for us, so we may come into fellowship with HIM. FATHER, SON, AND HOLY SPIRIT—THE THREE IN ONE GOD, THE GOD OF THE BIBLE—and into a true and genuine fellowship with those who know HIM.

So, what are you waiting for? Go before the LORD YOUR GOD and open your heart to HIM. HE IS WAITING FOR YOU. He may either send a genuine minister of His to you, or He may send you as a genuine minister to someone in need— knowing you will give HIM the glory and not expect recognition or fame for yourself.

> *He may send you out to bear the burden of HIS heart and strengthen others' relationship with HIM, all the while strengthening your very own relationship with the LORD your GOD.*
>
> **DEBORAH SUBASHINI RAJAN D.**

In the following chapters, names have been changed to protect the privacy of the individuals.

CHAPTER TWO

Compassionate Caring

Once I was traveling on a bus and I was drawn to a young person who I felt had emptiness in his life. He looked so dejected and lonely. I spoke a few words to him and gave him a bookmark with my address on it, which said: "I CARE FOR YOU!"

"Are you lonely, troubled, rejected, forsaken, depressed? Do you need someone to listen to you? Do you need a friend to pray for you? Has someone you trusted let you down? If so, you have a shoulder to lean on. I am available to help you, for once I was lonely, troubled, rejected, forsaken, and depressed, and Jesus met me at the point of my need. HE CARES FOR YOU!"

One morning, I heard a knock at my door. There stood this young man whom I had met on the bus! He said the bookmark had touched him, and he felt he could open his heart and share his pain with me. He shared how he had left his house and come to Bangalore and was staying in the waiting room of the railway station. He wept and told me about his pain and agony. He was emotionally disturbed. He said he was forsaken, rejected, with no one to care for him. His own parents never cared for him. This young man, Mark, said: "For much of my life I have been on a search for my identity, a quest for belonging."

Mark shared with me that one night, as he was on his way back to the railway station for the night, it started raining. He wondered how he would reach the station without getting soaking wet. He saw a church in the distance and went inside and met the Pastor.

He asked whether he could stay the night in the church. He said, "The pastor spoke to me for twenty minutes and then sent me away with a prayer." What Mark needed right then was God's protection and provision, displayed through the pastor of that church. He did not need a sermon, but a place to stay.

An unknown author made this poignant observation about how we fall short of the Lord Jesus' standards by acting according to our convenience: "I was hungry, and you formed a club to discuss it. I was in prison, and you stayed in church to pray for me. I was naked, and you debated the morality of my appearance. I was sick, and you thanked God for your health. I was homeless, and you told me about heaven's streets of gold. You seem so holy and so close to God, but I am still hungry, lonely, cold and in pain. Does it truly matter to you?" [Matthew 25:35-36]

All I could do was listen attentively and weep with him as he wept and at the end give him a hug. It was a spontaneous gesture.

I keenly sensed how he had missed out on of the love of a father. I told him how I was very close to my own earthly father, who loved me very much, but he died when I was very young. That shattered me. All along, I was hungry for love. At the funeral service, when my father died, I remember looking at his dead body and felt, "Oh, I will always miss his loving embrace!" I was longing for my father's love, and I missed it so much.

I was hungry for love and deeply mourned the loss of my father's love, yet how my Heavenly Father embraced me! And oh, what peace, satisfaction, inner healing and rest I found in Him—in His embrace!

Mark was in tears as he listened intently to my words, and they went straight to his heart.

We should let His love touch others. I love the words of Fawn Parish in her book "It's All about You, Jesus: A Fresh Call to an Undistracted Life."

She says, "You do not need any special credentials, any

talent, or any paperwork. Do you love Jesus? Do you know Him? All you really need are two arms and two lips. Your arms are needed for embracing and your lips for telling your personal story. How has Jesus been faithful to you? He will love the unlovely through us."

I just wrapped my arms around this young man, Mark.

I love this story that Fawn Parish goes on to tell in the same book.

Catherine Booth, a vibrant woman who co-founded the Salvation Army with her husband, frequently visited prisons. One day, as she entered a prison, she noticed a woman at the end of the corridor who was violently resisting being put into a cell. Catherine immediately proceeded down the hall toward her.

As she went, she thought, 'What can I do? Maybe I'll give her a Bible? No, she's too upset to read right now. Perhaps she might need some money? No, money will not help her.'

Before Catherine had fully settled in her mind what she was going to do, she found herself face-to-face with the matted-haired young woman. Instinctively she kissed her on the cheek and then walked away.

The next day when Catherine returned, the warden

told her she had to go visit that woman they had booked the previous day. This woman kept asking, 'Who was it that kissed me? Who was it that kissed me?"

Catherine found her and asked gently, 'Why do you ask who it was that kissed you?' The woman hesitantly replied, 'When I was a baby, my father left my family. We lived in a damp tenement basement, and my mother caught tuberculosis. When I was seven, my mother died. But, before she died, she took me in her arms and kissed me. THAT WAS THE LAST TIME BEFORE YESTERDAY THAT I KNEW ANYONE CARED.'

Sometimes unlovely people are just a kiss away from God.'

The only thing I could do to help Mark's situation was to ask him to stay with me. Instead of giving him a sermon, I wanted my life to be the sermon. I gave him a set of my house keys to make him feel loved. Mark said, "How can you trust me with your house keys? You don't know me! What if some things go missing from your house?" I told him that the things at home were not at all important to me, but that HE WAS!

This brought Mark to tears. "I've never had anyone do

anything like that for me, ever, in my whole life. I am a total stranger, and you are treating me like your friend, as your family member."

I love the words of a dear man of God: "There are routes we must travel to conquer inner space. You may have to go via the stomach, the wallet, the mind, or various other routes – whatever is necessary to get to the heart." Whatever is necessary, as Bill Miliken once commented, to learn the right to present Christ."

Mark stayed with me for a few months, and the love of Christ transformed his life. It did not take a sermon or preaching on my part, but God's love, which flowed through me by His grace. I remember one night when Mark never came home, and I was waiting on the balcony. He did not even call to say he would not be there, and I was worried. I could not sleep that night. Now tell me, who was Mark to me?

I had met him on a bus and gave him a bookmark. God brought him to my house and now he had become so dear to me that I was sincerely worried about him. That's GOD'S LOVE working in and through me.

The next morning when Mark finally showed up, I shouted at him saying, "Don't you know how much I was worried? Why did you not call? Where were you?"

Chapter Two

Mark was surprised, and felt wonderful to know that he was loved, and that someone was actually worried about him.

He said, "My own parents were never concerned about me. They did not care where I was. How is it then that you love me so much?" Mark knew the pain of being not wanted by his family.

I reminded him that this was the love of Christ. I told him, "You are God's beloved."

I remember making his bed, giving him breakfast, and then leaving for the day. I would leave enough food at home for him to cook and eat whatever he liked. At night, when I returned home, I'd share the day's experiences with him—all that the Lord did in and through me during the day. Then I would pray for him.

One day, he told me: "You never preach at or counsel me, you just treat me well and love me, and that impresses me so very much!"

I love Bill Milliken's statement: "People want your heart. But we have to give our hearts with no strings attached. We can't say, I'll love you if you'll come my way, if you believe what I believe. If you follow Christ, then I'll love you. We must remember He loved even those who did not love Him."

Michele Perry said in her book "Love Has A Face" that: "It is in this place of knowing Him that I become His love encounter to the world around me. I have nothing to give apart from that. It is a call of compassion where I live in Him, and He lives in me. It is there in that place of knowing His love that I can become His embrace to others."

As a child, Mark was hurting, and was filled with anger and hate. The stories of all he went through were very hard to hear. I felt I was called to love him out of all his hurts and pain!

l love the words of Michele Perry as she ministered to a child in deep pain, "Hate cannot stand in the face of love. The answer was to love her past the place of her pain and oppression, to become the face of His love. So, we held her and loved her and dodged her swipes. We blessed her and loved her and sang over her. One week, two weeks, three weeks. Love takes time. It is not to be hurried. Love stops.

Love is patient. Love suffers long and perseveres. We entered into the high worship of laying down our sleep, laying down our meager time alone, laying down our desires and even some of our needs for the sake of another. We died! Oh! Did we die. But, as we died, little by little she began to live. How did freedom come? Gradually, in an instant—I do not know. But one day she was different.

One day she was so filled with love that the evil had no more room. Love cost us, but it was worth more than we could ever give."

Mark shared that he had a dream of having an orphanage for children, and today, with much prayer, he is indeed running a home for children! Look how God works! Once Mark ran away from home and after having received the life-changing love of the Lord, he now picks up children from the streets who have no home! He is burdened to show the love of Christ to these children who are without a home and to care for them. God is using him in an amazing way! ALL GLORY TO THE LORD!

As I travel, I meet many precious people, each with a unique story. People are crying for genuine love—love that heals, that encourages! My heart is so burdened for the lost and the broken-hearted people, and I love to wrap my arms around their broken hearts.

May our lives be all about loving Jesus and loving people! Let our lives shine His light and shine His love!

STOP FOR THE ONE

I would like to close with something I heard one time that has always stuck with me:

"More of His voice in my ear. More of His tears on my face. More of His praise on my lips. More of his death in my life. More of His toil on my hands. More of His hope in my grief. More of His fruit in my service. More of His love for the lost."

CHAPTER THREE

A Night Out with God

It was a night I will never forget!

I was on my way home on my Kinetic Honda scooter after visiting my friend's house late at night. The air was cool; the road was narrow and seemed to go on forever. As usual my trustworthy gearless scooter was puttering happily along the tar road. After a while something felt wrong. The scooter was dragging as if a tire was going flat, and sure enough—it was! The tire was punctured, and I had only one choice. I got off my scooter and started pushing. I knew right then that I would have to push it all the way home in the dark and dusty night.

It was a long and lonely road. There were no houses around and the road looked deserted. I knew I was very far away from home, and I could not imagine having to push my scooter all the way to my house. I managed to push it for some distance, but pretty soon my muscles were aching and I was very tired. In all that time, nobody had traveled this road—I was all alone!

I was sweating and felt I could not push any further. I knew frustration could easily mess with my mind at this point since I had no other way out of my dilemma except to keep pushing one more step at a time. Something within me said, "God is with you"!

I was at peace. I felt God was indeed with me on this dark, lonely and tiring road. I felt an inward peace even though externally I was exhausted and still had a long way to go before I reached home. I paused for a moment and thanked the Lord for whatever purpose He had for allowing this to happen. This night's trial was not going to be easy, as I was going to discover soon.

Often, when we find ourselves unexpectedly alone, tired and in a troubling situation we tend to think it's an attack from the evil one. We panic. We worry. We start binding the evil in the name of Jesus. We easily give into the idea that every tough, hard situation is somehow orchestrated by the devil. That is so far from the truth. God allows situations in our life to prove His power on our behalf!

That was what I was soon going to experience. I felt confident that the Lord was watching over me despite the darkness that surrounded me and the physical tiredness that threatened to overwhelm me.

Chapter Three

I did not panic even though I had no one I could call to help me. Deep down in my heart I knew my heavenly Father had His eyes on me and knew the situation I was in. Oh, what an assurance and joy it is to know that even though we may find ourselves in the darkest moments with nobody around to help us, that the God who knows the stars by name also knows us personally and has said in the Holy Bible: "I have drawn you into the palm of My hand." We who are the children of God are drawn into his palm! Think about that for a moment. God has you safely secure in the palm of His hand. Can you imagine getting lost in this world without God ever knowing about it? There is literally no place that is beyond God's reach. He may not be physically visible to our naked eye, but He is ever presently there to help us.

Over the years I have gone through so many experiences that I have learnt to be at rest in Him, as time goes by. I can just simply rest in the knowledge that God is my Abba Father! He is my loving, heavenly Daddy! I have experienced Him working full time in my life. I have seen His mighty hand rescue me time after time. I have felt His concern cover me. I have been aware of His goodness as He gathered me to Himself. I have sensed Him favoring me with His faithfulness. I have encountered His love lifting me.

Now, strengthened with my Lord's presence, I began to push my vehicle with greater confidence. It's not easy pushing a heavy scooter when the tire is flat, and you've already pushed it a great distance. It was exhausting as I kept pushing but as I went, I was thanking the Lord and kept talking to Him. I whispered, "Lord, it's ok. Yes, I am tired, but it's ok. You do what You want in this situation. Just give me some extra strength to keep moving."

On and on I went, with my dialogue in my head with the Lord. After pushing for a while, I came to another road, and this one was well traveled! Vehicles were passing me, but no one stopped to help.

Apparently, God did not send anyone down that road to come to my aid. It might sound weird that God did not have anyone on the road help me. But you know, when God works, He often does things in a different way that is beyond our understanding. He has a bigger plan to accomplish, and our temporary inconveniences work for the greater good.

We can't figure it all out in our natural mind, but only in our inner man are we given the assurance that no matter what trouble or trying times we are going through, that God—the great Emmanuel who is with us—does what is best for us!

Chapter Three

My inner strength surged as I was filled with a deep assurance that God was indeed with me, and for a while I forgot my tiredness. I joyously broke into a song even as sweat poured off my face.

I sang, "No, never alone, no never alone, He promised never to leave me, never to leave me alone."

I kept pushing my Honda. Soon a hotel came into view, and my heart leapt for joy. Finally, some place I could safely park my scooter! I pushed my scooter towards the gate and asked the security guard if I could park for the night and pick it up the next day. To my dismay, he was rude and not cooperative. I kept calm. I did not react. I quietly asked if I could speak to the manager. Hesitantly he agreed and got the manager to come out to where we stood.

The manager was a young man, and he saw I was tired, worn out, and in serious need of help. My shirt stuck to my body since I was covered in sweat. I knew I looked as tired as I felt. I told him about my scooter's flat tire and how I had had to push it for such a long way. I asked if I could park my scooter there for the night. He looked at me with sympathy then said, "Okay, you can park your vehicle here tonight, but you have to pick it up tomorrow morning."

I felt God had prepared this manager to help me. I did not know why at the time, but I was sure God was in this. I asked this young man for his name, and he answered Joseph.

With tears in my eyes I said, "Joseph, I am a man of God and I just want to tell you that the Lord is so pleased by your kindness and willingness to help. He will surely bless you." Joseph smiled.

After parking the scooter, I started walking home. I could not get any bus or other means of transportation at that hour, so I kept walking. To my relief, God intervened, and a moving van stopped, and the driver offered to give me a ride home.

I got home and was so bone tired that I wanted to go to bed immediately. As my head hit my pillow, deep down in my heart I felt great peace. Heavenly calm and delight surrounded my soul. In the midst of a long night full of incredible hassle, I felt assured God had worked His plan. I dozed off to a peaceful, deeply restoring sleep.

The next morning, I went to the hotel and picked up my scooter, as I promised I would. Before heading home, I left behind a New Year's greeting card with a personal message for Joseph, the kind manager.

Chapter Three

After I returned home from the day's ministry, I checked my email and lo and behold I saw something pop up from Joseph!

He wrote: "Pastor, you thought your scooter tire got punctured by accident. No, God had a plan. He brought you to me, and that's why you had to go through that hard experience in the night. I have been in deep pain and agony. I was in tears. I had nobody to share anything with. I have been weeping and asking God for help. I was at the end of the road and the Lord saw my tears and sent you to me. Your coming was a direct answer to my prayers!"

Joseph went on to share his problems, and I prayed with him. The situation turned into a huge blessing for Joseph as I ministered to him through prayer. I was profoundly moved by this experience. It made me realize that my scooter incident was a huge part of God's plan for Joseph, and that allowed me to minister to another child of His with a problem that needed special intervention.

The Lord knew Joseph was in a tough situation and needed special help. He sent me there by very unconventional means. Oh, what a privilege it is to be a part of God's plan and to be used by him.

If I had called a friend for help on the night of my flat tire and long walk, I would have missed the unique opportunity to be able to meet and minister to this child of God in desperate need. Sometimes we have to go through hard situations for the Lord to accomplish His plan in our lives. Being a part of God's work is not always an easy thing. There can be a personal price to pay. It is the way of the cross. Without a cross there is no crown! We should always be available to God for His use. His eyes are searching to and fro throughout the earth looking for people who are available for Him to use. The rewards of our willingness will make all the momentary suffering worth it all!

There are so many people who are in tears, broken, hurting and wounded in body and soul. We need to be the hands of God to reach out and touch them with His love.

CHAPTER FOUR

Set Free From the Chains That Bound Me

This is the amazing testimony of Peter, a young man whom God delivered from a life that was headed into disaster, and totally transformed his life.

Peter shared this amazing testimony in a special meeting I orchestrated many years back, to show what an amazing God we serve.

It was amazing to experience watching all the church elders and believers, who had given up on him years ago, and witness in this meeting how the Lord took this youth who they all believed would never amount to anything, and wonderfully touched, delivered, saved, and transformed him.

STOP FOR THE ONE

Here is Peter's testimony, in his own words:

I sincerely thank God for giving me the opportunity to come before you all and share what the Lord has done in my life. I was born into a Christian family and God blessed me with God-fearing parents who truly loved me. I used to read the Bible every day and go to church regularly, but deep inside my heart was not in it.

During the last days of my school in 10th class/grade, some friends and I were tempted to try one small alcoholic drink. That small drink soon led to a daily habit. It became our routine to go to lunch break, have a drink and then have lunch. A friend of mine, who is also with me now in this meeting, would join me and we'd do all kinds of rubbish in school, most of which nobody in their right mind would ever consider doing. In school we were so bad that our teacher used to say we would never be able to graduate because we were always drunk and misbehaving in class.

By the grace of God, towards the end of the year 1994, I got baptized and the Lord helped me to pass my 10th. I still wonder how I cleared it! After that, I went to college and my parents thought everything was fine with me. My life supposedly changed after I was baptized, yet here I was back to how I was before I started drinking. Shortly after starting college, some

Chapter Four

friends asked me if I drank. I said that I had been drinking, but I stopped. They encouraged me to go out with them and enjoy their company and maybe have just one little drink. It would be fun, they said. I agreed to join them, and off we went. And before I realized what had happened, here I was, on just the second day of college, back to getting drunk and partying. This went on for nearly 2 years. If I missed a day of college, friends would call me and ask why I wasn't there. It was 17 kilometers from my home to the college, and where I'd meet my friends to drink. I would gladly go that entire distance just to meet with them and get drunk."

One day after the two years of bad behavior and hard drinking had passed, I found out that Christian worship leader Ron Kenoly had come to Bangalore and was there for a three day meeting. I had heard before that he was an impressive singer, so I thought I would just go and see for myself if it was true. I am sure that my going to see this man was a direct answer to my Mom and Dad's prayers and tears. I thought I would just attend the meeting and see what was in it for me. My brother and I ended up going together. Once we were there, my brother saw Brother Ravi Kapoor and introduced me to him. So, with my normal outward politeness but lack of caring inside, I met him and said it was nice to meet him. Brother Ravi greeted me warmly, then gave me a bookmark with his address and phone number on it. I took it and made note of the phone number. I don't remember what I actually did with it. The meeting ended, and after I returned to the college, I was in my own world again, drinking and partying with friends for three more months."

Shortly after that, I was in a club playing snooker, as I had done many times before. However, this time, in the midst of all that I considered great fun, I began to wonder what I was doing there. I distinctly felt as though I had no business doing what I was doing in this place.

I knew my life was not pleasing to the Lord as I had chosen to live it. I tried to forget these feelings and began to think on other subjects. Strangely enough, Brother Ravi's image came to mind, and I thought to myself that I would perhaps go and see what he might have for me. I called him and blurted out, "Uncle, I would like to meet you."

He simply said, "OK." He was going out that day and said to just meet him on the way.

As soon as I met Brother Ravi, I had the strangest feeling almost immediately that I could trust him and

Chapter Four

open my heart and share anything with him without judgment or condemnation. I ended up telling him all that I had been doing. The next day he called me, and we spoke for a while. On the third day my parents asked him to visit me at home. I got very angry, and I scolded my mother and father and demanded to know why they had invited him to come see me there.

I used to find it quite fun to mess with preachers and people who attempted to give me advice or counsel me. I liked to pull their leg, or treat them disrespectfully, yet I found I had no desire to do that with Brother Ravi. Something was holding me back, not allowing me to do this. As days went by, we became very close. I could freely and safely open my heart and share all my thoughts, feelings and everything with Brother Ravi and we became close friends.

Every day we would talk on the phone for a long time. I would meet him somewhere and we would just be together. I felt so close to him and was surprised to find something peculiar with him. He never once told me I should stop drinking or living as I was. He never talked with me about any of that but through his patient love, care and his prayers, the Lord began to touch me, and I began to change.

I was attracted to him. I loved to meet with him and spend time with him. He told me to come for prayer and attend the prayer meeting at his place. I agreed to try a meeting to see how I felt. I soon began going to his place every Saturday and actually looked forward to being there for every prayer meeting. I felt GENUINE LOVE as I saw how Brother Ravi was weeping and praying for so many. My heart started to soften towards God. I was convicted and touched by the love of God, which took me completely by surprise.

THE LORD DELIVERED ME FROM ALCOHOL!!!

I saw the power of prayer working a miracle in my life. I became a new creation in Christ Jesus! All the old desires and my lifestyle passed away, and everything became new and fresh. (2 Corinthians 5:17)

For once, I truly loved to attend the prayer meetings on Saturday instead of just going through the motions of acting religious, as I had before. I started going to church and everyone who knew the old me saw a new person and were amazed to see the mighty hand of God making my life new... transforming me completely. Not only was I delivered from alcohol, but the Lord strengthened me through Brother Ravi as he guided me to leave my old circle of friends for good.

Chapter Four

It could only be the power of prayer that brought me out from under the influence of them, for before all of us had been very close and spent much time together.

And now? It's been two and a half years since I had a drink, and I don't even feel tempted. I have God, who is my everything, and the memory of the prayers of my loved ones, my dad, my mom, and my brother, who earnestly prayed for me at the lowest point in my life.

Even though I was not faithful to the Lord during those years when alcohol ruled my life, He has incredibly blessed me and has brought me up in life, which I never expected. People thought I was too far gone, and well beyond hope, but God never gave up on me. There are still a few things to be changed in my life and I pray in the near future that this will happen. God will not let me down. He's already lifted me up.

My message to you is this: If the Lord was able to change me, He can change anybody. Nobody is too far gone to be out of His reach! The important thing was that I was willing to change, so it was easy for Him to change me and lead me onto the straight path. If there is anybody caught in this bondage, please believe me when I say you can easily be set free—provided you want to change.

> GOD is stronger than alcohol and through Him this terrible problem can be overcome. I thank God for bringing Brother Ravi my way and using him to change my life.

You heard Peter's testimony about how Jesus set him free from alcohol and brought him into His fold. Oh, the memories his story brings back to me!

I remember meeting Peter's brother, Martin, in a Christian library where he shared with me about his brother Peter and how their family was going through a lot of pain and agony due to his addiction to alcohol and resulting bad behavior. Martin asked me to visit his place and meet Peter.

Now, I know young people do not usually appreciate an evangelist visiting their home to counsel them without their permission, so I normally do not visit. Instead, I prayed and asked the Lord to arrange a meeting that would be according to His plan and in His time. A plan like this always works best since only God knows when a heart is prepared and ready for such an encounter.

My heart carries a burden for youth and when hearing about Peter's story, I immediately sensed he was in pain, and my heart went out to him.

Chapter Four

I began to pray for Peter. The power of prayer works mighty miracles when nothing else might be effective.

I had faith that God would send an opportunity my way to reach out to this young man. It was definitely this, the answer I had been praying for, that brought Peter to Ron Kenoly's meeting. Peter would normally not have attended such a meeting and God also positioned me to attend as well. He, the Lord, brought the two of us together.

When Martin saw me, he was so excited that I would be able to meet Peter and counsel him. I went up to Peter as Martin introduced us. I smiled and spoke a few words to him, then left the bookmark with a message and my phone number with him. Martin was bewildered and said privately, "Uncle, I thought you would spend more time counseling Peter? You spoke less than five minutes with him before walking away, and who knows when you will get the chance to see him again!" I told Martin that I spoke just what the Lord wanted at this moment in time, and we can be confident that God will do the rest. We only need to keep praying.

Later when I began to meet with and minister to Peter, I sensed that nothing I could say or do would change him. That was God's job, not mine. Only the Lord can change a hardened heart!

My job was just to love him, pray for him and let God bring about the transformation in Peter's life. Humility, knowing we desperately need help and cannot receive it on our own, captivates our Lord and He faithfully comes to the aid of those who honestly admit how desperately they need Him.

Our weakness, in fact, makes room for His power in our life as NOTHING else can. Praise God!

I developed a friendship with this troubled young man. I wanted to know the reason WHY he was getting drunk and acting as he was. Something was very wrong in his life, and I prayed for wisdom on how to proceed with him. I let him know that I was concerned about him, but more importantly I took the time to get involved personally in his life. I deeply cared about everything that concerned him.

Soon, I realized he was feeling as though nobody genuinely loved him or cared enough to truly understand him. He needed to see real love in action, not just be told casually that he was loved.

Peter seemed rough and uncaring on the outside but was actually very warm and tender inside. He kept that side fiercely hidden from the world.

Chapter Four

H.S. Vigeveno once said: "To love the unlovely, to keep on loving, to love unselfishly, this is a gift of God."

Even though I had other things that needed to be done, I wanted to be sure Peter knew he was important, very important, to me. As he began to comprehend the value I had placed on our friendship, he would call me, and we would speak for a long time every day.

I have seen over and over when dealing with young people that most of them act as though they are complete in themselves and lacking nothing, yet inwardly they are fiercely seeking acceptance and need to feel wanted. We make an impression if we show real interest in them and spend time with them personally.

I gave dear Peter time whenever he needed it and met with him whenever he wanted a cup of tea or to share a meal together.

Sometimes he would look at me and say, "Uncle, why are you spending so much time with me? Am I so important?" I would simply smile and heartily reply, "Yes, you are!" I meant it. He knew it. And his heart began to soften.

I agree with what Kenneth C. Haugh stated in his book "Christian Caregiving, a Way of Life," that "A Christian caring relationship touches the whole person. It is not limited to the physical, or the mental, or the social, or the emotional or the spiritual. Christian caregivers follow the example of Jesus Christ and cannot avoid being holistic to the best of their abilities. Christian caregivers understand that the whole person needs ministry. Christian caregivers know that God alone is the one who takes broken individuals and makes them whole."

Peter's transformation was not due to my unique personality or charisma, but only by my willingness to be used by the Lord to reach a hurting young man. It was God who worked in Peter's heart and brought the change. I was only His vessel.

After Peter received Jesus into his heart and experienced the dynamic power of God that set him free, the pastor and elders of the church were in awe of the marvelous work of God in this young life!

For quite some time they were simply unable to fathom the change in Peter because many of them had given up on him, after witnessing his alcoholism and the bad choices he was making with his life. Peter, on the other hand, knew quite well the change that had taken place within himself.

Soon, his own heart began to ache for others who were still struggling with addictions as he had been for all those years. Many young boys in the church needed help, love, and prayer, and Peter brought quite a few friends to me. The mighty hand of God delivered many from alcohol and drugs. Thank you, LORD!

Today Peter has been blessed with a good business and a devoted wife and two lovely boys. He is immersed in the church that he is part of, and God is using him in ministry. He freely shares his persuasive testimony about how the Lord Jesus set him free. I praise God for blessing Peter with a godly life partner, and revel in the fact that God is using both of them in a special way for His kingdom.

Seeing the way God is using Peter, whom so many people gave up on all those years ago, makes me just stand in awe of the One who worked such a transformation in Peter's life.

I strongly believe that those who have been told they will never amount to anything are often the most thankful and the most willing to reach out and help others out of the same circumstances, once they themselves have been pulled from the depths to which they had fallen.

Today, Peter is a testimony of this!

His personal business is thriving. He is serving in a variety of ways in the church and is ever ready to step in and help anyone with whatever kind of need they may have. God has definitely blessed him with a tender heart that goes out of the way for the one who needs a gentle touch and encouraging word.

I love what a precious woman of God, Janet Kennedy Buffaloe wrote, "I love God's Redemption, Restoration… NEW beginnings and our message out of our mess! YOU and your story are His miracle and someone else's HOPE. Pause and ponder… "

In my ministry, I've come across many drug addicts and alcoholics, and the Lord led me to put some into rehab. With Peter, all he needed was just the LOVE of Jesus, and the POWER of PRAYER, since he was open and receptive to receiving inner healing. Peter was longing for love and when I reached out to him with genuine care, he was deeply moved. He saw I cared enough to fully listen, get involved with him, and to deeply care. I believe Peter received practical care right where and when he needed it, and he was made whole and transformed by Christ's love.

How true is the statement made by Kenneth C. Haugk: "Christians are responsible for care; God is responsible for cure."

I find most of the youth today have been misled. They see others' manipulation of people to get what they want. They witness all manner of hypocrisy. They become hardened, for survival's sake. They have seen others get hurt and they themselves have also felt the sting of betrayal, so they learn quickly not to trust people. They cover themselves with a hard shell for protection from the rest of the world—no one gets too close.

We must be able to break through that impenetrable facade with love and perseverance; showing them that we are not just trying to take advantage of them in some way, or manipulate them into doing what we want, at their expense. We need to first gain their trust by simply listening and loving without judgment, an agenda, or time limit.

We also need to prove ourselves faithful when they share their pain. What they tell us should go no further, to anyone else but the Lord. We would add unimaginable anguish if we'd gossip about the things these dear youth have told us, no matter how far-fetched or terrible it may be.

A betrayal of what they confided would just reinforce that hard shell and make it nearly impossible for them to trust anyone ever again.

Through that consistent love and faithfulness, they will be open to the Word and Father's love. This is how I work. Love them with the love of Christ and continue to love them as time goes by!

My heart burns with a passion for the YOUTH of the world. My heart aches and cries to the Lord for their young lives. So much pain at such a young age! They are without direction, floating aimlessly and trying desperately to stay afloat in a world that seems cruel and uncaring.

Just a few days ago I was telling some people not to give up on their children. These children are into drugs and alcohol and have taken up with the wrong company, trying to find the "real thing."

My friends, we have the REAL THING! We have the One who will reach right through all the confusion, hardness, rebellion, hurt and need for love, and Who will redeem their lives and hearts like no one and nobody else ever can—and He is JESUS!

This is why my heart cry has been for the Lord to raise up fathers today, those who will sit at His feet and be filled with His love and wisdom from above. Physical and spiritual fathers who will stand in the gap for the youth and show them love beyond what they have known before, that which can only come from God!

That's what I do, for I too have been hurt by others, well-meaning as they were at the time. I know the pain! I sit at His feet and receive His love to share with the unlovely and wisdom to deal with them in a way that will help them to come out of whatever their addiction or other issues might be.

Someone once asked me, "How do you go about dealing with an addict? What kind of counseling do you give them?" That is not what I feel led to do. I answer this question by saying up front that I am not a counselor, nor have I taken any training to help with their problem in that way.

God has gifted me differently. I'm a good listener and I CARE! Because I genuinely care, I can get to the root of their issues to know what their hidden problem is: where they are hurting and why. I care for them deeply with the love of Christ.

They share with me their deepest hurts and wounds, and I listen, understand, and feel with them, then allow the Lord to work and bring the inner healing that comes through loving them and praying for their needs. When I deal with an addict, I just listen! I try to understand the feelings behind their words.

The core issue, where the root dwells of all that is wrong, is what we need to get to. Once there, we must show them there is a way through this, no matter how bad things have gotten. We can never get to a point of no return with God.

He is there waiting for them and loves them as much as ever and is gently calling them back to Himself. They need to realize, as Peter did, that there needs to be a change. The road to healing can begin with their recognition of this.

Romans 12:1-2 says: *"Therefore, I urge you, brothers and sisters, in view of God's mercy, to offer your bodies as a living sacrifice, holy and pleasing to God—this is your true and proper worship. Do not conform to the pattern of this world, but be transformed by the renewing of your mind. Then you will be able to test and approve what God's will is—His good, pleasing and perfect will."*

Not one of the troubled youth that I have ever met grew up as a child dreaming to be an alcoholic or a drug addict or a thief, or whatever else the enemy has coaxed them into. No! They were each born with a special destiny and every single one, just like you and I, were created for greatness. God has incredible plans for each of us and His will is that we fulfill those plans for Him, for His Kingdom, for each other and for ourselves.

Chapter Four

Jesus tells us that He came to destroy the works of the devil and to give to us a life of abundance. This is not something we have to die for to receive in Heaven. No! Jesus declares in His prayer, "Father, who art in Heaven, Holy is thy name. Thy Kingdom come, Thy will be done, on earth as it is in Heaven...." Yes, on earth NOW, not later in the hereafter.

Our children must learn this! We must tell them how wonderfully special they are. God created each of us in His image. This in itself can be so hard to grasp, because it is difficult to comprehend that the God of all the universe cares so individually about each and every one of us!

The other thing to think about is that God created us, and we are one of His masterpieces. WOW! The youth need to hear this.

They need to know how valuable they are, how much we need their individuality, their energy, their unique ideas, their hands and feet. Each one is so important. They are amazing! They are a special generation who can change the world with GOD, by whom all things are possible!

Let us never look down upon a young man such as Peter for the awful things he was doing.

Rather, let's look at all the Peters on Earth through God's eyes and see an extraordinary gift to the world, just waiting to be unwrapped. What a tragedy when these talents and ideas never get to be brought out and their destiny is never fulfilled. We must make the effort to reach out and let them know they are loved and have so much to offer!

CHAPTER FIVE

Search Hard to Bless Someone!

In 2nd Timothy, Paul mentioned an amazing man named Onesiphorous, who was a lesser-known person in the Bible.

The only mention of him was in three verses, found in 2 Timothy 1:16-18: *"May the Lord grant mercy to the household of Onesiphorus, for he often refreshed me and was not ashamed of my chains, but when he arrived in Rome he searched for me earnestly and found me—may the Lord grant him to find mercy from the Lord on that day!—and you well know all the service he rendered at Ephesus."*

Onesiphorous blessed Paul in three ways:
- He refreshed Paul,
- He was not ashamed of Paul's condition, and
- He searched hard to find Paul, until he found him.

Onesiphorous's influence on the Apostle Paul was so profound that he released a blessing on him as he wrote about him.

He invoked God's mercy on his household. We don't know for sure if this man's household believed in Christ or not, but it looks like they did not. Paul called on the Lord to be merciful to his family, knowing the mercy of God is a valuable blessing to have in our life. The book of Lamentations 3:22-23 says "The steadfast love of the LORD never ceases. His mercies never come to an end, they are new every morning; great is Your faithfulness."

His mercies are new every morning! Because of His mercies we have not perished. James 2:13 says that judgment without mercy will be shown to anyone who has not been merciful. Mercy triumphs over judgment! There's not a day that goes by in our lives that we don't mess up. We fail both God and people so many times. We deserve to be judged but God's mercy overpowers the chastisement we have earned by our actions. His mercy keeps us from what we should receive.

God's mercy was invoked to protect and save the household of Onesiphorous all because of one man's caring nature, good works, obedience and willingness to look for the good in others.

Chapter Five

Onesiphorous did that. He knew the situation Paul found himself in, yet he still did everything he could to reach out to him.

Are you like that in your life? Do you sincerely care about others? Are you interested in caring, even if it might take a lot of effort? Have you ever thought about those people that nobody else cares about?

They are totally alone. They have no one to call and talk to. They sit by themselves in a room, waiting for a phone call, an email message, a Facebook text or a knock on the door.

ANYTHING to let them know someone cares enough about them to take time out of their day to contact them. Have you reached out to such people? They could be hurting, lonely, depressed and in very difficult circumstances. They may well be desperate for someone's encouragement and kind words.

But you may say—How do I know where they are? How can I find them? I don't have time. I have a busy life. Yes, it may all be true that you are not in a position to care, and you may not have the time. But let's go back to what Onesiphorous did. None of us knows what his personal situation was like.

The only thing we know for sure is that he made the time and searched hard until he succeeded.

Those few words, "he searched hard" are powerful. Onesiphorous was not required to visit Paul. For all we know, he could have been a busy man himself with enough of his own problems to deal with, as most of us are. But because of his caring heart he searched hard to find Paul, regardless.

His desire to help another person meant going the extra mile, searching hard, until he accomplished his goal.

That's the kind of people we need. People who search hard to help others. People who go the extra mile. People who take the time, regardless of personal cost.

Have you searched hard to help someone?

Or did you give up halfway and not bring much needed encouragement to that person who could have used it?

Go that extra mile.

Look and see what you can do to make a difference in someone's life. Be the hands and feet of Jesus to someone. Get up and do something to bless others. Be caring. Be a shining example of love to those who need it most.

Chapter Five

Think about this! Matthew 25:35-40 says: *"For I was hungry, and you gave me something to eat, I was thirsty, and you gave me something to drink, I was a stranger, and you invited me in, I needed clothes, and you clothed me, I was sick, and you looked after me, I was in prison, and you came to visit me."*

Then the righteous will answer him, "Lord, when did we see you hungry and feed you, or thirsty and give you something to drink? When did we see you a stranger and invite you in, or needing clothes and clothe you? When did we see you sick or in prison and go to visit you?" The King will reply, "Truly I tell you, whatever you did for one of the least of these brothers and sisters of mine, you did for me."

The Bible is saying that what you do for one of the "least of these"—brothers and sisters in need—counts as though you did it for God Himself!

Isn't that amazing? Jesus says I was hungry, thirsty, a stranger, naked, sick and in prison. Paul was in prison and Onesiphorous visited him.

In effect Jesus is pleased that Onesiphorous, by visiting Paul, not only blessed and encouraged Paul, but blessed Jesus by his caring about Paul.

STOP FOR THE ONE

We touch God when we reach out to the poor, lonely, needy, sick, depressed, and suicidal. Our society is full of lost people looking for love and kindness.

I hope this day you will think of someone who is depressed—perhaps call someone who is hurting, visit someone who is sick in the hospital, or all alone and languishing in their house with no one to care about them. God is in them. Jesus is in them. Make that call. Find that person.

Search for them till you find them, regardless of how much time and effort it may take. May God bless you. May He have mercy on you and your family on the day of judgment as He remembers all you have done for Him!

CHAPTER SIX

When the Lord Told Me to Take a Left Turn

While on my way home late one night, I was about to make a right turn towards my house, but the inner voice of the Lord asked me to turn left.

I knew it was very late, and the left turn would not lead to my house, but I obeyed the Spirit of God anyway and turned left.

As I kept riding my scooter down that deserted road, I saw a young man seated on his bike. The Lord said, "Go and minister to him."

I parked my scooter and walked towards him. I could see he was very drunk. I thought he looked lost and anguished. I stopped and asked if he needed any help.

He screamed back, "Who are you? What do you want from me? I have nothing to give you, leave me alone."

I gently put my arm around his shoulder and said, "I want nothing. I just want to tell you that I am concerned about you. It's very late at night and you must go home."

He kept screaming, "What do you want from me?" I said, "I am God's love to you."

He looked at me and cried, "I want nothing to do with God. He doesn't care. If He did, He would not have taken my wife and child away from me. I don't believe in God." He started weeping profusely. He was literally shaking with pain.

I just listened to him and let him pour out all the hurt and anger that he had in his heart.

I kept reassuring him that I was there to help him. I told him, "I understand how you feel. I can identify with your pain."

Maybe he never heard such words before. He started weeping even harder and proceeded to tell me that in the midst of his anguish, he had been sitting there contemplating ending his life.

Chapter Six

He told me he was very lonely and miserable and there was no one for him to talk to.

He wept as he explained how his wife and daughter had left him and the heartbreak and depression it had caused. He was so fed up with life, he said, that he went to a bar and drank until he was very intoxicated; he intended to then climb a tall building and jump from there to his death.

It was at this very crucial time that the Lord sent me directly to him. I knew at this moment that my left turn was indeed a command from God to reach out when it was most needed. God was taking special care of this man at his loneliest and most desperate hour.

I told him, "From now on you are not alone in the city of Bangalore. You have a brother to care for you, someone who loves you—and that's me."

I realized that what he needed at that moment was not a sermon but a compassionate shoulder to cry on. He needed to feel accepted, understood and loved.

What some people normally tend to say to people like him is, "You have sinned against God. You are drunk, and the Lord is angry with you. Because of your bad choices, you're suffering now."

STOP FOR THE ONE

But, alas, what people need in their loneliness and pain is not a sermon, but you. YOU are the sermon, and your actions are the words. Thankfully, God gave me the grace to show His love to him. I believe people respond when they know we are genuinely concerned about them—when they know we are not trying to condemn them or make them feel bad about themselves.

I quietly and patiently listened to him as he poured out his heart and was weeping bitterly. He was deeply hurt and wounded, and I wept with him. I let him weep out his pain.

After a while, I put my arms around him and whispered a prayer for him. God's love and comfort to him flowed from me in that hour of his great grief. Afterwards, he shared his story with me. I inquired where he lived, then asked if I could take him home. He was ready to go home because God's healing presence had calmed his disturbed heart, and His embrace through me, had brought peace.

He got on his bike, and I rode alongside him on my scooter. We came close to his house, and he stopped and said I could go, as he felt fine now. I asked him if I could leave him at his door, but he refused.

I kept quiet.

Chapter Six

He gave me his phone number and asked me, "Will you call me? Will you keep in touch with me? Will you come to see me?"

I hugged him and said, "Yes! I surely will call, because it was Jesus who brought me to you."

I left and the next day I called him, as I promised. He thanked me and asked me to visit his house that evening.

I asked for his address, and he said, "You know where I live because you dropped me off here at home last night." I explained that I had just left him near the house, but had not actually come up to the house. He was confused.

He said, "After you left me, I kept riding my bike towards home, when suddenly I hit a tree and fell unconscious. It was then that you came, lifted me up and rode with me to my home."

I could not believe this at first. How was it that I did not know his house if it was I who had helped him to his house?

For a moment, I was confused. Then it dawned on me that this had to be an angel who lifted him up and took him home. Amazing!

Our loving God had sent an angel to rescue this young man! I was so overjoyed to know that the hand of the Lord was caring for him in a very real, physical way. Beloved, that is our God. He reaches out when no one else is around.

I visited him later and continued meeting him often, and I showed Christ to him by simply loving and caring for him. Later, I was able to lead him to the Lord. He asked me for a Bible and started to attend church as well. I believe the Lord accomplished His purpose in and through our meeting. By His grace, I obeyed the Lord in reaching out to this hurting man, to love and minister to him, give him a Bible, lead him to a church and continuously pray for him.

Praise God for He is a God who is always on time. He reaches out to rescue His children right when He is most needed, from the clutches of the evil one.

God never comes too late in our life. His timing is perfect—always. Jesus has come to give life and life abundantly. It is the devil who has come to kill, steal and destroy. The devil planned to kill this young man, Srinivas, by leading him to commit suicide, but the Lord had a different plan for him. If I had not been sensitive to the voice of the Lord and obeyed Him instantly, young Srinivas would have died that night!

Chapter Six

Thank God, He always wants to reach out and touch those who are in need. The problem with us, His children, is that oftentimes we are not sensitive to His voice. How lovely it would be if only we would listen for and hear His voice, and then do His bidding.

Beloved, we need to obey His voice! Yes, even when it sounds risky at a very late hour in the night, and we have other plans of our own! If anyone would have seen me with a drunkard at that hour, on that deserted road, you can imagine the talk about me. But for me, it was a matter of listening to God and doing his will, regardless of what may be said about me. I had to hearken to the Spirit's still, small voice and go in search of that one distressed soul that needed the Lord right at that time.

Praise the Lord, for He is moving and working miracles outside the four walls of the church! God is calling us to come out of the church building and into the streets. The disciples walked the streets, reaching out and touching many lives. May the Lord move in His power through us every day and at every place our feet touch! God is waiting for us to agree with Him for miracles everywhere we go!

Even though it sometimes seems like a small deed, when the Lord tells us to GO, we better obey, and right then! A life might depend upon our obedience!

We should be the hands and feet of God. We should call someone and encourage them. We should speak a word of cheer, say a word of praise and a word of encouragement to someone in need. We should let others know that we care about them with the love of Jesus. This is the result of living a genuine Christian life.

Mother Teresa once said: "Love does not measure; it just gives. We can do no great things: only small things with great love. Little things are indeed little, but to be faithful in little things is a great thing." She further added another important truth, "Being unwanted, unloved, uncared for, forgotten by everybody—I think that is a much greater hunger, a much greater poverty than the person who has nothing to eat."

Imagine being so unloved, uncared for, and forgotten by others that it is a much greater poverty than to go without food! We need to show the love of Christ in a real way, meeting genuine needs. God is love.

In John 13:34-35, the Lord Jesus says to Peter, *"A new command I give you: Love one another. As I have loved you, so you must love one another. By this all men will know that you are my disciples, if you love one another."*

Be available to the Lord whenever He needs you.

There are multitudes of people around each one of us who are hurting and in pain. When we show the way to Christ's love, we are tangibly walking out the love of God.

I pray that we will always run into someone in need and share the joy that we have, then leading them to the One who gives that joy—Christ Himself!

Oh, how I long to be His arms, His feet, and His hands to the hurting and needy people around me!

I have prayed to the Lord time and again, "Lord, may my life be spent reflecting, radiating and living your indescribable love."

STOP FOR THE ONE

CHAPTER SEVEN

The Healing Power of Listening

One day I received a call from a woman who said her son, Rahul, had locked himself in his room and refused to let anyone in.

I could hear the anxiety in her voice. This woman had gotten my phone number from a dear friend of mine who had shared with her about me and my ministry. Rahul was her younger son and the family desperately needed help and prayer. They wanted me to come and do something about Rahul's situation.

I told them I would be there soon, and upon reaching their house I sensed commotion. The parents told me that their son might get very angry and uncooperative if he found out they had called me. They were not believers. I asked them what their son was good at or enjoyed doing and they replied that he enjoyed working on his computer.

After praying for wisdom, I knocked at his door. No reply. I knocked again and kept knocking, while calling out his name. After some time passed, the door finally creaked open.

The young man, Rahul, looked at me warily from behind the door. I told him that I had heard he was quite gifted with computers, and I would love to see some of the work he had done. As soon as he heard me say this, he felt less threatened and told me to come back tomorrow. I went away praising the Lord for this opportunity and praying for wisdom to know how to proceed with him.

I met him the next day and he began to show me the amazing work he had done on his computer. I told him how very good it was and how I was impressed. It became obvious to me that he needed to feel appreciated.

I got the feeling that he had faced a lot of rejection, so I asked him to teach me how he did some of his computer work. I had no real interest in computers and was finding it difficult to understand much of what he was showing me. I did not enjoy computers as he did, but I knew this was something especially important to him, so I attempted to learn. I wanted him to understand that I truly cared about him!

Chapter Seven

During those visits with Rahul, I never once told him about God and His love or my testimony or anything related to the Bible. I just spent time with him. I let him get acquainted with me. I just spoke words of encouragement to him. I was simply trying to get to know Rahul on his terms.

LONELINESS

After a few days, in the middle of our conversation, I looked at him and said that he looked very lonely. Tears formed in his eyes, and he stopped what he was doing and asked how I noticed that. He went on further and explained that yes, I was correct. He was very lonely and felt he had no friends. I asked if I could be his friend. He wept openly and accepted my offer.

I could sense the Lord's hand touching this young life. God had worked in Rahul's heart and prepared him to open up and share his loneliness and pain with me. He told me how he had been rejected. He went on to share about his deepest hurts and wounds. When he finished speaking, I sat quietly, knowing I had no great words of wisdom to offer.

We both sat in silence for few minutes. Then Rahul began to cry. I sat with him, keeping company with his tears, and still said nothing.

After a few minutes passed, Rahul said, "I have kept all my pain and hurt deep inside my heart, and this is the first time I've cried in front of someone. I could never be myself with anyone."

With tears he said, "You've helped me. You touched me so much. Thank you, thank you."

The silence had changed something inside of him. In my ministry I make it a point to listen to people. There are times I say nothing but inwardly will be praying for that person. I simply listen to what they have to say and let the Lord speak to them.

I love the words of author Bonnie Grove in her devotional book, "Being The Stillness": "There are astounding lessons to be learned from the act of listening. I have learned that listening is an act of love. It is not passive; it is intentional, engaging with the heart and mind of another person. To listen, you must turn off all outside distractions; say "no" to the world rushing by you. A sacred act of deliberate silence and meaningful pause, listening helps people clear a space in their life, heart, and mind in order to simply 'be.' Our listening is an important gift and I am learning to make it my first response. Through listening I want to provide the stillness God speaks into."

Chapter Seven

That's the ministry the Lord has trained me for—to be a listener. Henri Nouwen once said in his weekly meditation, "The Spirit of Jesus Listening in Us" that, "The Spirit of Jesus in us listens in us to all who come to us with their sufferings and pains."

A NEW FRIENDSHIP

I saw true healing occur when I attentively listened to Rahul and sat in silence and was fully present with him. All I say to a friend in deep pain is, "I AM HERE WITH YOU, YOU ARE NOT ALONE. I UNDERSTAND YOU AND YOUR DEEP HURT AND PAIN. I AM HERE, PRAYING FOR YOU."

There began a friendship with him. Rahul was touched by my love and care since this was something he had not experienced much of before. I had yet to tell him that this was the love of Christ that accepts, understands, listens, heals, and satisfies. I found out which food Rahul was fond of, and I would call him to join me for a lunch that I knew he would enjoy. Soon, Rahul would call me and ask if he could meet me.

Even though I might be far away in some distant area busily ministering to someone, he would insist, "I will come wherever you are. Distance does not matter. I just want to see you."

And he would travel far to see me and just BE WITH ME. He was a person who had totally isolated himself, not wanting to see anyone but now He began to look forward to seeing me and spending time together.

In the beginning this young man was not willing to open his door and talk. Now he loves to spend time with me. How did this happen?

Was it because I am a special, wonderful person?

NO. It's GOD'S LOVE alone that can penetrate each and every heart, no matter how closed they might be.

Only He has the key to open all hearts and we need to be available for Him to work through us. Love is very powerful, and it will melt every hardened, unyielding heart.

"We are to BE His love, GIVE His love, LIVE His love," says Kathy Troccoli, from her book "The Colors of His Love." This is true!

There are many times when we fail to love or care about the ones God brings our way. We tend to act super-spiritual, ready to give our advice; impatient, ready to judge but not be people who would truly listen to the ones who are deeply hurt and wounded.

Chapter Seven

Do you realize sometimes they just want us to be with them? Listening to them?

I hardly speak to the ones in the deepest pain. I have nothing to say to them that would mean as much to them as a listening ear, which I love to do.

Henri Nouwen in his weekly meditation, "Listening as Spiritual Hospitality" says this about listening: "True listeners no longer have an inner need to make their presence known. They are free to receive, to welcome, to accept. Listening is paying full attention to others and welcoming them into our very beings. The beauty of listening is that those who are listened to start feeling accepted, start taking their words more seriously and discovering their true selves. Listening is a form of spiritual hospitality by which you invite strangers to become friends, to get to know their inner selves more fully and even dare to be silent with you."

In one of their books, authors Dee Brestin and Kathy Troccoli stated: "'If the church were a heart, its current failure to love is like a massive heart attack. We, as arteries, get clogged with judgment, hate, pride and gossip. How can His lifeblood flow through us toward each other, let alone into a world so desperate for the love of Christ?"

THE NIGHT OF DEPRESSION

One night around 2 AM, Rahul became deeply depressed. I got a call from him, and he told me how he was so very lonely and that no one loved him. He felt as though he was good for nothing and could not take living that way anymore, so he no longer wanted to live. He wanted to speak to me before dying and now that he had—he could die.

I told him that the Lord Jesus loved him. He was precious in His sight. He had carved him in the palm of His hands. Rahul replied that he was tired and just did not want to live. I could sense he was at the end of his rope. I tried all I could to encourage him. I told him how deeply I loved him and how dear he was to my heart and asked him not to make this decision to commit suicide. He refused to listen. I kept praying, asking God to give me the right words to reach him as I spoke to him, and for God to touch his heart in a way He alone could.

After a lengthy conversation, I realized he was still not willing to listen.

I prayed harder, then told him that he can go ahead with his plan. I would not stop him. I asked if he loves me and he said, "I do. You know I love you, brother. You mean so much to me and that's why I called you."

Chapter Seven

I asked him if he would do me a favor before dying. He said he would.

I told him that I wanted to meet him only once and after I do, then he can go ahead with his plan to die. He agreed. I would visit his house early tomorrow morning and spend just a few moments with him. After that, he could go ahead. He said okay.

SAVED FROM SUICIDE

I thanked the Lord for Rahul's willingness to meet me, and the tears flowed as I prayed hard the rest of the night, burdened for Rahul. True to my word, early the next morning I went to see him. He cried and cried upon seeing me. I allowed those tears to flow. I too cried. I said nothing. I was just with him and stood out of God's way as the Spirit touched him and brought healing and deliverance. The Lord rescued him from the spirit of death. I asked him later what had happened to him that night to make him talk like that. He shared that he had been so down and felt terribly helpless and hopeless. One thing especially that he spoke touched me. He said, "You told me, brother, that you are there for me and you always understand how I feel. You said to feel free to share my heart with you. You will always accept me as I am so I thought that before dying I would call you and share my heart and tell my brother how hopeless I feel. I had hoped you would be there as you promised."

I was so happy and told him that he can always feel free to be honest with me and share whatever he felt without fear of being judged or rejected. I reminded him again that I will understand and be there for him—to accept, care, encourage and lift him.

People are hurting and they have no one to open up and share their hurts with. Nobody they can trust with their feelings and struggles. Satan takes advantage of this and sets a trap for them, causing them to eventually lose control and give in to his schemes.

We as believers in Christ should be there for others and speak words of encouragement to them in their hour of need. We can thwart the enemy's plans for destruction if we simply care enough to BE THERE for those who are hurting.

I believe when we show pure love without an agenda, that it is hard to resist. I just wanted Rahul to sense that I sincerely cared for him. I was by his side when he needed someone. I think my presence brought healing to Rahul and gave him comfort.

The Lord touched his heart as I sat there with him, and

Chapter Seven

made all things new.

I read once that sometimes we give our thoughts on salvation and that's good, because we want the person to know about the Savior Who alone can make all the difference. Yet we don't care about the person's state of mind and heart and being wise concerning what to speak, allowing the Lord to work.

I have seen numerous times in my experience with many people that we will get a lot more respect when we show we really care, and we sincerely listen. The more we love our brother, the more we will show His mercy.

I cared so much about Rahul and out of my love for him I spoke with him for a long time over the phone that evening. I forgot about sleep and prayed earnestly the rest of the night for him, knowing that when I see him in the morning the Lord would have worked in his heart.

We are to have God's love and simply BE His love. It's easy to show love and speak a few words of encouragement then pray over someone on the phone then go to sleep, knowing we have done what was required when someone shares their heart's burdens with us. But it is something altogether different, and much more difficult to actually BE His love! To be His love means we get more intensely involved, more deeply burdened and at times even go without sleep or other comforts, to help the other person who is in pain.

I wanted to reflect the heart of Jesus to Rahul, and I knew this was literally a life-or-death situation. When we are so filled with His love, we do not let the person go without making a difference.

If I had been content to speak a few words and pray for Rahul over the phone and then go to sleep for the rest of the night, I believe the next morning I would have received the news that Rahul committed suicide. Love takes sacrifice and if we have God's love, we will gladly sacrifice our comfort at times, to make the difference in a person's life.

God brought Rahul my way. He knew when the time came where Rahul's life would hang in the balance that I would obey Him and step out of my comfort zone to bring him back from the precipice, into renewed life.

God brings people my way and I just want to love on them. Jesus said, *"Love one another as I have loved you"* (John 15:12). I pray that we will always keep our minds full of how much He has loved us and live our lives full to overflowing with the love of Jesus.

I love what Kathy Troccoli says: "We must not settle. We have access to His power. We can continually drink from the river of His love. Why don't we take advantage of this? He will take us to higher and greater places if we would trust Him to do so and make ourselves available to Him."

So, what happened with Rahul? Praise be to God! Eventually I was able to share with him about the One who loves him so much that He gave His life for him on the Cross.

He died not because He had no reason to live, but because by His death all of us can have new life in Him and experience that love that never fails! Rahul accepted the Lord Jesus as his Savior and today he is a new creation in Christ Jesus.

The old things have passed away. Behold all things are new. Rahul now faithfully attends church and fellowships with others, where before he had been alone and depressed. God has blessed him with a good job and he is happy and joyful in Him.

STOP FOR THE ONE

CHAPTER EIGHT

The Compelling Power of Love!

If you know me personally, you know I am very fond of reading. One day a dear friend told me about a library that is open to visit, where I could sit and read. He said they have a good collection of Christian books. I was thrilled!

This friend took me there, and introduced me to two of the librarians, who just happened to be brothers—both of whom had come to know Jesus from a Hindu background. In just a few days, we became close friends.

I began to frequently visit the library and enjoyed reading books by my favourite authors, and also spent time with these two dear brothers. I felt God was at work here and had a BIG plan in this divine connection with these men, this library, and me! So many people came in for solitary peace and quiet, to sit and read a book at their leisure.

In the process, God opened a wonderful ministry for me as I bumped into many of these people in our shared times in the library.

The Lord, by His grace, helped me to counsel and pray for many.

One such time was when a man named Dharam "just happened" to see the library's board on the gate and decided to come in. I was sitting nearby at the time, reading a book. Dharam approached one of my two librarian friends and shared that he speaks only Hindi. My friend brought him over to me and introduced us. What a divine appointment this was, with Dharam!

He sat beside me and began to share with me about himself. He was a dentist and was staying nearby, close to the library. He told me he is from Punjab, then asked about me. He was surprised when I told him that Punjab was my mother's hometown, and he was excited that I too came from there. He asked to know more about me. I shared my testimony with him, how I came to know the Lord Jesus from a Punjabi background.

Dharam was very surprised to find someone who had left the Hindu faith, personally experienced the love of Jesus and was following Him. He showed keen interest as he listened to my story and was clearly amazed.

He said he had to leave then and inquired when I usually visit the library. I told him that there was no specific day or time that I came, since I came as the Spirit of God leads and as I am able.

In just the short time we spent together that day, he had felt comfortable with me and said he would like to meet again. We began meeting in the library as we could and shared a short time of fellowship.

In one of our times together at the library, I told Dharam that I host a prayer meeting at my place. He was interested and asked if he could join in. I replied that it would be great to have him there at the meeting, which was held every Saturday from 1:00 PM-4:00 PM.

Dharam told me he would come for only about an hour, arriving around 2:30 PM and leaving by 3:30 PM, if that was okay. I told him that was fine.

I could see that he wanted to come secretly, and quietly leave before the meeting ended because he did not want to meet anyone. It is so important to be sensitive towards people, handling each situation with the wisdom of God.

I could have told him strictly that the meeting starts at 1:00 PM and he needs to be there on time and not leave until the meeting is done at 4:00 PM, but I try to always be discerning, and handle each person very delicately, tenderly and wisely.

Dharam started coming to the Saturday meetings and I loved it when he sang the Hindi and English worship songs along with the rest of us. I would pray for him but not mention his name, since I sensed he would not be comfortable with people knowing about him.

I would just pray, "Lord, thank You for bringing my dear friend here, whom You enabled me to meet in the library."

The fellowship and prayer were making a big impression on him. Dharam would not miss a single Saturday's meeting, yet he still did not break his routine of quietly arriving late and leaving before the meeting ended, to avoid having to speak to anyone else. The situation needed great wisdom and care, so as not to make him feel uncomfortable and maybe stop attending altogether.

I made sure Dharam understood he was dear and precious to me, and that I cared for him. Over the years, I have learnt to be patient with the Holy Spirit's work in the life of the one I'm ministering to. I have many Hindu friends and I deeply love them.

Chapter Eight

They mean a lot to me and I desire very much that they would come to know Jesus. This would be so wonderful, however if they do not give their heart to the Lord, my love for them will remain the same. They are precious to me and they are precious and loved by Jesus whether they personally accept Him or not.

It is vitally important to accept people as they are, from other backgrounds and beliefs. We should see the person and love what we see, and not look at what background they have or what religion they belong to, then decide whether to love them.

I have learnt to love the person, and in our conversations, I never inquire about their religion or background. I respect them and show Jesus' love to them.

I love the words by Kathy Troccoli in her book "The Colors of His Love": "Do we have sensitivity, gracious timing, and respect for another's beliefs? We are often more concerned with the "spiritual state" than with trying to understand or get to know them.

We don't know their background, their religion, their culture—we may not even know their names—yet we quickly present our agenda." Jesus has asked us to simply go to people and let them know He loves them.

STOP FOR THE ONE

He never told us to put anyone down or hurt those people of other faiths by telling them that what they believe is false and incorrect and Jesus is the only real way to be saved and go to heaven. Yes, it's absolutely true that the Bible says there is only one way to salvation and that is through Jesus Christ, who sacrificed Himself on the cross and purchased us by His blood that He shed on the cross of Calvary.

However, He does not want us to share the good news in such a way by telling people they are lost because they follow a false god and we are saved because we believe in Jesus. I was lost and separated from God at one time and was searching for Him.

I tried Hinduism, Buddhism, then Sikhism and after not finding what my soul was searching for, I became an atheist and stopped believing in God altogether. After all of this, I had an encounter with Jesus and found my heart had become filled with His love, joy, and peace—and I was not the same from that moment on. All things became NEW.

I remember before I was a believer in Jesus that a few Christians had approached me and said what I believed was wrong and that I must leave my beliefs and all I had faith in, to believe and accept their Jesus into my heart and life.

Chapter Eight

I was hurt when they put my beliefs down, and also as they made sure I understood loud and clear that only their way was right and I must leave my way and come to Jesus. These people had good intentions, trying to save me. What they were saying was the truth, but their approach was terribly wrong. They needed to convey the Good News with love, without offending the other person for whatever he believes or follows.

This is how I have learnt to be sensitive to people of other faiths, sadly—by being hurt myself by others' words, however well intended they were meant to be. I have dedicated myself to be very careful to never downplay other beliefs, and to speak in such a way that will only glorify JESUS and lift Him up. Jesus said, "If I be lifted up, I will draw all men unto me."

I remember reading about a Christian who told a well-known Hindu guru that "Jesus lives." The guru replied, "Where? I don't see him in you."

Isn't that tragic? Are we as followers of Jesus more concerned with trying to convert an unbeliever from their "idolatrous" religion than to speak gently with respect, concern, and love for that person?

Sometimes followers of Jesus tend to present the religion "Christianity" without sharing Jesus, the Savior.

Jesus did not come to Earth to create a new religion called Christianity. Instead, He said "Come to ME." "Follow ME." Our Lord is not the God of Christians but of all mankind! He came to save ALL, regardless of their religion, background, or lifestyle.

When Christians are truly following the teachings of Jesus, we cannot help but share His love with everyone we meet and feel burdened with genuine concern for the pain of those around us. We choose to honor each person even if their life choices are much different from our own.

Yet so many people have instead been deeply hurt by those who are Christians. They are turned off and completely closed to the idea of Jesus and His love, since some of His sincere followers have been acting quite unlovingly and in their haste to bring in the lost, they forget their Lord's gentleness when dealing with people.

Yes, unbelievers may be living a life full of sin, and yes, they need to be delivered from that, but our approach can very easily turn them from the Lord instead of to Him.

This must not happen! We must cease from practicing a religion and instead focus on following Jesus.

Chapter Eight

Fawn Parish in her book "It's All About You, Jesus" says something so true: "I fear that often we are only nice to people in order to convert them.

When they do not show any signs of responding, we move on to someone else more receptive. We must ask ourselves, "Is my heart toward a neighbor only soft because I perceive they might become a Christian? Our tenderness towards people must be because God's unfailing love is towards them. We are not responsible for their response to God. We are responsible simply to love. Someone once said, 'Love them until they ask you why.' That is the best counsel I have heard."

We must meet people directly at the point of their need, yet also allow them to be themselves and let the Holy Spirit work in them! All we are called to do is to be full of God's love—and let His love spontaneously flow through us to the ones He brings our way.

I just loved dear Dharam for who he was and accepted him as he was and never preached to him. I allowed the love of Jesus to work through me, knowing that this love is immensely powerful. That love changes lives!

Bob Johnson in his book "Love Stains" said something that I love: "When seeing a person who is broken, our natural reaction varies from giving that person a comforting smile to saying a silent prayer. More than likely, that is exactly what the Father is doing in that moment.

He isn't preaching to them about repentance. He is comforting them with His love. Our job is to be Daddy's love in the moment. More often than not, that does not look like giving a gospel presentation or leading a person in the sinner's prayer. This is not ignoring the person's need for salvation. It is loving without an agenda. A true taste of Jesus—a divine appointment in that person's timeline—will give that person one more reason to seek after Jesus."

We are called to preach through our lives. Most times this preaching may not involve quoting Scripture or leading a Bible study, but just being available to those who need us. I love to spend time with people and to get involved in their lives; to be myself and be real. I feel this makes it so much easier for them to accept us, knowing we have accepted them.

Through this mutual respect and trust, they are then comfortable enough to open up and share their heart, knowing it will not be betrayed or hurt.

I met Dharam again in the library and he asked if I would be interested in having a cup of tea with him.

Chapter Eight

He liked my company and was wanting to spend more time with me. Am I such a special person to draw people to myself like this? It is not me. When people feel God's love through us, they will be drawn to us without knowing why. This feeling becomes stronger as time passes until they finally MUST know what is so different about us!

However, with many Christians it is the other way around. When they meet someone and share about the Lord, they rush things and tell them we want to meet them again, give them a Bible and invite them to church.

Do not misunderstand me. ALL THAT IS GOOD. However, if we feel the person is not showing enough interest, do we just leave him and move on to the next person? That's really sad. Jesus never does that. If he had done that to me, I would not be here today sharing about Him and His love.

God's love is unconditional, with no time limit. No matter if it takes a person a short time to come to Him or many years—He will be there patiently waiting for us, to welcome us into His family.

So Dharam and I went to a restaurant and Dharam revealed that he had dedicated his life to serve in an ashram.

For those of you who do not know, an ashram is a place where a group of Hindus live together away from the rest of society, or a place Hindus can go to pray and meditate. Dharam lives in that ashram.

He told me that he has been part of this ashram for many years and also follows the teachings there. But he has yet to find peace even though he is regularly doing meditation and following what the ashram says to do for his spiritual journey. In spite of living a very disciplined life, he had not yet found God and still felt emptiness within.

He also shared that he was attracted to me and my testimony and felt peaceful whenever he attended the Saturday prayer meetings at my place. He said he was moved by the way I am burdened for everybody and prayed with sincere tears.

He wondered why I have such overflowing love for ALL. I told him that this is the love of Jesus, flowing through me. Jesus has deeply impacted my life and His love flows through me to all.

Oh, how much the Lord has impacted every part of me with His divine love! How can I keep it to myself? What a privilege and honor it is to be able to share His love with everybody.

Chapter Eight

Dharam began to enjoy not only the meetings on Saturday, but also the fellowship with others as the Lord freed him from being quiet and keeping to himself. He started to stay until the end of the meeting.

He would talk with everyone, introducing himself as a dentist from Punjab but keeping the information that he stayed in an ashram to himself. Dharam became especially interested in the 82-year-old woman who was my dear mother, when she became lost in worship and sang Hindi bhajans (worship songs).

One Saturday he met my mother personally and felt so welcome, so much at home, as he received a hug from her. She told him, "My son, it is so wonderful to have you over for prayer!" She shared her life's testimony with him. He saw such joy in my mother that he was overwhelmed. They developed a close bond, which made him even more attracted to Jesus.

Isn't it wonderful the way the Lord has divine meetings set up for people? Dharam could relate to my mother more than others would be able to, because my mother was also a devoted follower of a guru for many long years but did not have peace. She found her God, and in Jesus Christ also her complete peace, and was now an ardent and devoted follower of Him.

Then came a time when Dharam did not visit me for 2-3 weeks, nor did I receive any call from him. I did not have his contact number because he told me before that the ashram people do not allow anyone to call from outside. It really bothered me and I was very concerned about him. I decided one day to go to the ashram and visit him to be sure he was okay. I knew they do not allow any outsiders in the ashram, but I prayed and went anyway.

God knew I was disturbed and worried since I had not heard from him, and I know He heard my prayer.

When I reached the ashram, I spoke to them in Punjabi, their native tongue, and told them that I too am from Punjab and I came to visit my friend Dharam. To my surprise, they did not question me at all, and allowed me to go and visit him in his room. Do you realize how impossible this usually is for an outsider to be allowed inside the ashram? They are extremely strict, but when we pray and trust the Lord, He makes ALL THINGS POSSIBLE.

One of the staff led me to Dharam's room and I knocked on his door. When he opened the door, he was shocked, then great joy filled his face. The first thing he asked me was how I was allowed in. I told him that God wished for me to check on him, so no one could stop me.

Chapter Eight

I told him that I was quite concerned about him since he had not come for 3 weeks, and also did not call. Dharam said he was feeling sick so he could not come. And because he was not able to leave the ashram, he had no way to call me.

He was so moved that I took the time to check on him. He said that in today's world no one cares for one another. He mentioned that I was not even a relative of his, yet I took the risk of coming to check on him. I told him that Jesus loves him and He is so mindful of him.

I am only the Lord's vessel, available for Him to use to reach out and love and care for His precious beloved children, of whom he is one. He had tears in his eyes.

In all of the stories in this book you may have noticed that I have only one message—that we are called to simply LOVE. Be concerned about others. See people with His eyes of love. Be sensitive to how people feel. Let people know you value them. How my heart deeply hurts as I see so many people doing a lot of counseling, lecturing, and preaching sermons, but actually show VERY LITTLE LOVE. This approach pushes people away from the Lord, it does not draw them to Him. It can cause them to react defensively. Caring from the heart will not only help but will heal and bring restoration to the person once they realize they are loved.

When I looked around dear Dharam's room there in the ashram, I could see the Hindi Bible and Hindi testimony books that I had given him there on his table. It warmed my heart to see how much interest he had in reading them, by keeping them there.

I could have taken a casual attitude with Dharam. He had not been coming to the Saturday meetings, and was not calling me. Maybe he was no longer interested in coming or was restricted from leaving the ashram.

I had given him the gospel and showed him the love of Jesus. If he was no longer interested, some would say it was his choice, so I will not pursue him but rather only pray and let God bring him back. Many of us do this, and by doing so miss out on truly reaching someone. It is easier to think this way.

We all have other things we could be doing with our time. I have learnt to be more sensitive to the Holy Spirit and not lean on my own understanding. Jesus reached out to people. He went where they were. I am following in His footsteps when I go in search of the ones He leads me to, and I keep pursuing them when they disappear for a while.

Chapter Eight

It's His love that compels me to do this, for He pursued me when I needed Him the most. Taking time out of our busy schedule and reaching out is difficult or awkward sometimes, but it makes a lot of difference to that person, and also brings healing as they realize we care enough to follow through with them.

The person we go in search of and reach out to is deeply moved as he sees real love in action—someone caring so much for him, and in Dharam's case, someone who has taken a big risk to come and see him.

Those at the ashram could have been rude to me, or could have scolded me and sent me away, since nobody was allowed to see anyone inside. Everybody knows this. I could have told a big story of how I know him and how am I related to him. Instead, I chose to

be faithful to God and obey Him. As I did, He cleared the path for me to be successful on my mission! There were no questions or obstacles to overcome, to be able to enter the ashram and meet with Dharam.

When we are obedient to God's leading, He takes care of everything, down to the smallest detail, so it all goes smoothly. It did not matter to me if a friend, believer, or pastor saw me entering the ashram.

STOP FOR THE ONE

The news would have been spread that Brother Ravi is going into a Hindu ashram, and we all know such news travels fast. Such gossip is enjoyed by some people who would think I am living in compromise, both serving the Lord Jesus but also seeking spiritual enlightenment in a Hindu ashram.

By His grace, He delivered me from worrying about my reputation, and what people think of me. I do not care what people think or what they say. We are called to be a God pleaser and not a people pleaser.

All I want to think is what my Jesus thinks and as He guides, I will obey. I love to be busy doing my Father's business!

I have no time to ponder what people think, feel, or speak. We must leave them be and keep on doing what we are called to do, for we serve Him, and not them.

I am busy doing what I so love doing—reaching out and loving people with the love of the Lord.

The devotional book, "The Word For Today," had this statement: "Jesus left the comfort of heaven to walk the road of human need. He didn't set up a throne in each town and say, 'This is My place; if you want to see Me come here.' No, He went to the marketplace. He went to the fishermen's boats. He went to people's homes. He 'went through the towns, preaching the gospel and healing everywhere.' (Luke 9:6) He has called us to GO and show His love and care for people, heal the hurting, wounded, broken, physically sick and mentally disturbed. There is need all around us. All we need to do is GO where He would lead and get busy loving people with the love of Jesus."

After my visit to the ashram, Dharam kept coming to the prayer meetings, worshiping along with us, listening to His Word, and enjoying the love of the Lord and fellowship with His children. He was drawn closer to the Lord. Dharam found true peace and meaning in life through Jesus Christ and he began to follow Him and His teachings.

One day, Dharam told me that he shared about me, my testimony and ministry, with a dear friend of his, and this dear friend wanted me to visit him and pray for him. He also told me that this friend had asked for a Hindi Bible. So, one evening I went along with Dharam to visit his friend. Upon stopping, I asked Dharam where the friend's house was, because he had stopped my two-wheeler outside a Hindu temple. He replied that his friend is the priest in this temple. We went inside the temple, to his friend's room.

What an awesome opportunity God gave me to enter a temple and share with the priest about the love of Jesus.

I shared my testimony, prayed for him, and handed him the Bible. He was delighted that I visited him and was very thankful to me for coming. It was such an amazing experience!

What I loved the most was that not only did Dharam taste the Lord Jesus and found He is good, but he shared with his close friend how he found peace and purpose in life after he accepted Jesus as his personal Savior. This got the interest of his priest friend, who then wanted to know more about this Jesus who brought peace, meaning and purpose into Dharam's life.

Once we experience God's love, we cannot remain silent. We want to share that love with others!

I love the words of Tommy Tenney in his book "God's Secret To Greatness," where he states: "He is looking for people who will accept His commission to seek, serve and to save those who are lost. God wants us to venture beyond the four walls of our worship centers and steepled church buildings to take His light into the darkness and become His hands of mercy and love extended to those who do not know Him."

Chapter Eight

I also remember once when Brother Daniel, a precious man of God who was physically challenged, and very dear to me, was promoted to glory. I used to invite this dear man of God to share God's Word in the Saturday meetings. I let Dharam know of his passing, for he was acquainted with him from the meetings.

Upon hearing about his sudden homegoing, Dharam immediately came to visit me because he knew how close I was to Daniel and though he could not attend the funeral service, he was there throughout the memorial service. Look at Dharam's love for the Lord, love and honor for His servant Brother Daniel, and his love for me as he stood with me, comforting me!

How this deep love of God spreads from person to person! In the days to follow Dharam called me often to inquire about me and speak a few simple words of concern and comfort.

Bob Johnson said in his book "Love Stains" that: "There is only one hero who I want to pattern my life after: Jesus. He had an uncanny way of reaching people WHEREVER they were. He didn't try to convince them of something. He simply met them and gave them a taste of Himself. Every person He came in contact with experienced Him in a different way because He knew their hearts and ministered to them accordingly. Jesus didn't have a formula or a method that He used to help people; rather, He listened to His Father, moved in obedience, and ministered outside the box. If you want to touch people with Father's love, it is vital that we also become one with God so that we can move according to His heart."

Let me clearly say that it's ALL ABOUT JESUS. I am so humbled to see how God sent Dharam my way and He, who knew Dharam's heart, met him at the point of his need. I was only a vessel, "available" for His use, for Him to utilize to reach dear Dharam.

Dharam tasted the love of Jesus and found what he had been searching so long for. He began to tell others, "Look what Jesus has done in my life—and if you open your heart to Him, He will reveal Himself to you and your life will never be the same."

CHAPTER NINE

He Saw a Different Kind of Love

For many years, I have had a ministry to visit the sick in the hospitals and pray for them. This includes visiting the Baptist hospital twice a week to pray for the patients and minister personally to the doctors and staff, as well.

On one of these visits, the Lord led me to meet an American girl named Becky who was working in the physiotherapy department of the hospital, and we immediately struck up a friendship. She was moved by my testimony on how I received Jesus from a Hindu background, and how I am now serving Him full time.

Every time I would visit the hospital, I made sure I took time to visit with Becky and have a time of fellowship with her.

After a few times, she felt she could trust me, and she opened up and shared about a Hindu boy named Ashok whom she had recently met.

She confided that he was devastated and deeply hurting because both of his parents had died in a tragic accident. She asked if I would be willing to meet with him and if she could give him my phone number in hopes that I could reach him where others had failed.

I replied, "Of course! Please go ahead. I am available and would love to be an encouragement to Ashok."

In the Bible we see that Jesus made time to meet with people in need, and He specialized in bringing healing and deliverance to the broken and wounded. I have learned personally that, like Jesus, sometimes these people do not always come at a convenient time when we have no plans or anything else to do.

Yet if we chose to not become available for the one He brings our way today or not take time because we are too busy with our own agenda, we will miss out on the heavenly assignment He has for us.

Who then will bring the much-needed healing to the one He has entrusted to us? The opportunity may be gone forever. May I never turn my back on anyone He has sent my way!

I received a call from Ashok one day, and I asked him to visit my home. I have no doubt that it was Becky's

Chapter Nine

prayers for him that gave him the courage to agree to come and meet me. It soon became very obvious that he was in incredible pain since he had refused to speak to any of his friends or family who tried to reach out to him and help him work through his sorrow.

He had isolated himself, feeling nobody could understand the depth of his anguish, or do anything to make him feel better.

Soon after speaking with him on the phone, he agreed to come and visit me. When he appeared at my door and I looked into his face, the deep pain in his heart was evident in his eyes. I welcomed him into my house and did what I could to make him feel comfortable. I had soft instrumental worship music playing in the background, and I invited him to make himself at home. I asked if he would like to have tea or a cold drink.

He politely refused. I told him that I'd not had tea yet, thinking we could have some together. He agreed and as I went to the kitchen to make our tea I said again for him to feel at home and know he is in a friend's house and to just relax and enjoy the music.

After I brought in our tea, we drank it slowly and got to know each other a little better for a few minutes as we chatted casually.

Soon, I became quiet and allowed him to talk freely and share whatever was on his heart. He, with tears in his eyes, shared about how both his parents had died two years ago due to an accidental fire in the kitchen. This incident shattered his life, and he was so deeply shocked and broken that he stopped believing in God.

I told him that where there is deep hurt like he is experiencing that there will be tears as he relieves the memories of this terrible time. Since we all have feelings and love others—especially family—deeply, there is no shame in being open and sharing our deepest emotions. He began to tell me more in detail what had happened, and I did nothing but listen.

As he spoke more, his confidence grew and soon he was sharing the ache that was so deep and entrenched in his heart for which he felt there was no answer or healing.

I sat in silence with him. I was fully present with him, and gave him my full attention. I did not speak a word. All I did was allow him to talk, and feel and share his deepest pain. As I listened, my own heart cried out in anguish as I sensed Ashok's agony. Yet at the same time I was astonished as I watched him begin to transform. Even this simple act of being heard and not judged or interrupted was gently helping him onto the road of healing!

Chapter Nine

Writer Ren Bazin says, "A remedy for the evils of our time is the gift of yourself to those who've fallen so low that even hope fails them."

I have seen repeatedly in my experience with people that we will get a lot of respect when we show we sincerely care and will really listen. I had simply encouraged Ashok to feel at home and did all I could to make him comfortable. This was my task.

The Holy Spirit was then able to minister to him because I stayed out of His way. There was nothing I could have said that would have helped, encouraged or comforted Ashok because of the level of turmoil he had inside.

The soft worship music I had playing was relaxing and felt safe and non—threatening. Yet at the same time the atmosphere was charged with the Spirit's presence. I was able to join with Ashok, especially since I truly understood his pain, having lost a family member in a terrible accident.

My 20 year old brother Raja, who also happened to be my best and dearest friend, had died in a drowning accident as I watched, helpless to save him—so I knew the piercing pain and agony Ashok was currently experiencing.

STOP FOR THE ONE

Ashok was astonished to see my own tears as I was crying along with him. He thought he had come to meet a pastor, which he felt meant that I would share with him some words of comfort and encouragement and then send him away with a prayer, but his impression was wrong.

Instead, he experienced someone who was personally identifying with his deep pain, as he was encouraged to be the one to speak and share the burdens in his heart without my interference. I only sat silently and listened.

In my ministry, I have learned not to ask the wounded person how he feels. Instead, I put myself into their situation and try to understand their pain from their perspective and not my own. I only speak the words the Lord gives me and am very careful not to add any of my own because this is always a mistake.

Even those words of ours that we feel are perfect and wise can sometimes cause pain, since we can speak with judgment and not love. God's words on the other hand bring healing!

I do not have the answer as to why my brother died that tragic death at such a young age, so why would I presume to have the answer as to why both his parents lost their lives in that horrible fire?

Chapter Nine

So, I just listened. I cried along with him because I understand that there are times when we are not called to say anything. God, instead, commands us to simply *"weep with those who weep"*. [Romans 12:15] I believe it is our presence, and us being fully present, that can best give comfort to the one who is grieving.

Perhaps you have been wounded by a well-meaning but very misled person in your own life?

It is quite painful to others when we give explanations and answers to those people in pain, out of our own understanding—and actually end up only making things worse. I remember once many years ago when I had a serious accident, and my left foot was crushed under the tire of a bus. I had multiple fractures and underwent major surgery and was in the hospital for one month.

One evening a pastor came to visit me. It brought great joy to my heart when I saw him come into my room to visit with me because I had been feeling depressed and could have greatly used some comfort and encouragement.

He sat beside me and opened his Bible, then proceeded to preach to me and inform me how my life was not right with God and because I was disobedient and harbored sin within my heart that this accident was due to God punishing me. He went on and on about the sinful condition of my life, then he finished by praying in the same manner that he had preached.

As I am sure you can guess, after he left, I was feeling much worse. I had needed a word of comfort from the Lord!

If the word this pastor had shared was truly from the Lord to me, that I need to get right with God and walk in obedience to Him and not grieve His Father-heart, I surely would have received that and truly repented and got right with Him, surrendering afresh, and requesting the pastor to pray over me.

However, the words he shared were from his own interpretation and not given to him through the Spirit of God. Instead of bringing relief and restoration, his words threw me deeper into despair and discouragement.

I can still remember praying through the added sorrow that night, "Lord, I am already in deep pain and all I needed was a word of comfort to strengthen me, and someone to say that I am not alone and whatever has happened that I can know You are with me and will turn this around for my good, and Your glory. This pastor

Chapter Nine

did not speak words from You. Lord, help me to always remember tonight and how these words cut me deeply, when it was healing that I needed. Help me to learn from his mistake, so that I will speak only what You give me to speak to those You call me to visit who are sick or in a bad situation."

What people in the deepest pain need is not a sermon, but someone who will sympathize with them as Your Son Jesus did with others while He walked this earth; to feel their pain and to be Your comfort and encouragement to them.

"So, Lord, I ask that You perform a deep work in me so when I visit the sick or the hurting, I will be very sensitive to Your Spirit and be careful what I speak. If I do not receive a word from You to share with them, just help me be silent and only listen and pray for them. May I never feel I am qualified to give them a word on my own which I feel is what they need to hear in their situation. May I be from this moment on nothing of my own, and all of You and from You."

Today I can thank God for the precious pastor and the words he spoke because all has worked out for good! God has used this well-meaning man's mistake to make me more sensitive to the tears and cry of the heart of those who are sent to me.

And it has also allowed me to be more discerning to give them a word ONLY from the Lord. I care practically for them and journey with them in their pain, but I leave the rest to God. We should ask the Lord to give us His heart, His love, and His patience for His hurting children.

When He makes it clear that we are to speak, we must not share just a few superficial words, say a quick prayer, then leave. The Word of God is powerful and effective and can reach deep into a hurting soul and provide the exact answers that they have been searching for! We must never place a time clock on these divinely arranged meetings. A soul could be lost forever if we decide we have better things to do than spend our time with them, loving them as they need us, where they need us, and however long they need us.

Ron Hembree said in his book "The Speck In Your Brother's Eye" that: "To effectively communicate with people, we must first learn to be sensitive to them and also love those who are lost in their own loneliness. Sacred sensitivity is the key to effective evangelism."

All I told Ashok was that he is not alone. I simply asked him if he would accept me as his friend. He was deeply moved. I shared with him the love of Jesus that cares, listens, understands, heals and satisfies.

Chapter Nine

Michele Perry says, "We become expressions of His love to the world in the places of their pain."

I prayed with Ashok and afterwards could see a difference as God's peace and serenity became visible on his face. As I said amen, Ashok immediately asked which church I attend on Sundays and when I told him, he asked if he could come with me. I was completely taken aback seeing the sudden change in this dear man.

You see, Ashok was an atheist! He had been angry with God for so long, and was full of pain thinking this is all he would ever know, and now? He could not wait to come to church with me. I at once recognized this as nothing short of the transforming work of the Holy Spirit. I was so overjoyed knowing Ashok was on the path to complete and total healing.

That very next Sunday he did attend church with me. There he met my sister, Renu, who also accompanied me to church every week. He was delighted to meet her and found her easy to talk to, which was miraculous since he had disconnected from all his relatives after his parents' untimely deaths.

He continued coming to church every Sunday with us, and after hearing the message he had many questions that he would ask me about the service.

I would share with him what I knew and the things I was not sure of I said I would check into and let him know later. He was touched that I was not trying to make him feel that I know everything but let him know that I too am still learning.

I was very careful in dealing with and replying to his complex questions. I did not want in any way for him to be hurt again or take a step backwards in the growth he was experiencing. With much prayer and wisdom, I dealt with each question as it came along.

At this time, Ashok was working for a very good local business. One day he said he wanted to take Renu, her son Amit, and I out for lunch. We were pleased to take him up on his offer and had a wonderful time of fellowship together.

I could see the joy in his heart because he found a family in us. He had previously held a different impression about "religious" people such as a pastor or evangelist, feeling that they would only be talking about the Bible and spiritual issues in a very impersonal way.

He discovered quickly that he had found a brother and friend in a man of God, with whom he could be himself without fear of judgment or ridicule and he was accepted, understood, loved and cared for.

Chapter Nine

In Renu, he found a sister who also cared for him as I did, so he felt we were truly a family, and he was delighted every time we could spend time together. We were not only preaching to him but we were "normal" people, interacting with him in whatever topic came up in our conversation, and making him feel at ease.

After attending church for one month, Ashok visited me at home and confided in me that he had made a deal with God that he would attend church for one month and see if he feels a change and gets the answers to some of his questions. If he did not, then he would stop going. He smiled and said that his heart had indeed changed and he will continue to attend the church! I was most happy to hear this.

We do not have to try to force people into believing Jesus, but just show His love in practical ways and allow the Spirit of God to work.

He will amaze us by what He alone can do once we take ourselves out of the way. I never insisted Ashok must come to church, neither did I tell him not to miss any of the Sundays. I just left the choice up to him and prayed for him. Now, because he had received the touch of God that heals and transforms, he himself refused to miss a Sunday and would come with love and reverence for the Lord.

STOP FOR THE ONE

He sat beside us and worshiped along with us and so attentively listened to the message and prayed.

All I did was pray that his spiritual eyes would be opened to experience the full love of Jesus and that the Lord would meet him, heal him, and give him a brand-new life.

Once Ashok told me, "I have experienced religion before, and after my parents' accidental death, I stopped believing in God. Yet what I have seen in you is a different kind of love and that has attracted me to you. That is what gave me the desire to know the God you follow and also go to church, because this love that I saw in you was contagious. Just being with you made me feel as though you put courage into me. I feel peaceful when I am with you."

I explained to him that Jesus, the Prince of Peace, lives within me. Jesus, the great Encourager is always with me, so His peace and encouragement are imparted to him through me when he is with me. It is never about me. Left to myself, I could not do as I do with His guidance and help.

It's ALL ABOUT HIM, not me. Jesus has impacted my heart and life so deeply with His love, that I cannot help but BE His love to others.

It is His unconditional, selfless, sacrificial love that flows and forgives, heals and transforms any and every one who comes to Him. His love can reach anyone at any time, but one needs to be open to receiving His love. Ashok was open to receive His love, and that love changed him forever.

I reminded him that I am only a vessel God chose to show him His love. I am privileged and thankful to Him for choosing me, but had I not made myself available to Him, He would have used any one of His other children to minister to Ashok.

So, it is truly ALL ABOUT HIM. I told him both of us can give God all the praise and glory."

The words by Julia C. Loren came to my mind: "In a world that glamorizes the achievements of men, Heidi Baker shuns the spotlight when she speaks in conferences, those attending tend to see and hear more of Jesus and less of her. Her joy is to fade into the background and let Jesus take over."

This is exactly my desire—to let people see and hear more of Jesus and less of me as I desire to fade into the background and let Jesus take over and receive ALL the glory for all that has been done.

Once Ashok told me that he wanted me to visit one of his friends and pray with him. His friend was feeling much of the same way Ashok himself was, and he was also sick. I replied that I will pray and let him know when we can visit. He said something that struck me. He said, "Even just your presence in his house will bring great peace and comfort to him. Being with you and spending time with you makes one feel so relaxed and peaceful, and every anxiety and disturbance leaves."

It was a great surprise to hear that this was what he experienced when he visited me the first time, and how he immediately wanted more of this peace, and agreed to attend church.

He not only received a comforting reassurance that he was loved and cared for, but he felt and experienced the instantaneous peace of Jesus and the presence of God. This brought such calmness and rest to him after his soul had been in torment for so long.

How true it is that we are carriers of His Glory—privileged children much loved by our Father and honored to be His temple. As His available servants, we share that love to those He sends us to.

Wherever we go, we carry His presence and the atmosphere changes because of it.

Chapter Nine

Others can feel this shift, and are drawn to the difference of Him in us and ultimately, they are drawn to the Lord Himself. Only in His presence is there the fullness of joy that has eluded mankind for ages. In His presence, there is freedom, healing, and deliverance from all that enslaves us.

John 1:5 says, *"The light shines in the darkness, and the darkness has not overcome it."* When we enter a place, whatever is not of God will immediately leave because the darkness cannot bear His light in us.

This is our heritage as children of our Heavenly King! We are light bearers, and that light can be seen for a great distance.

One example of this was the time I visited a family for prayer. I was invited into their home and sat in a chair. A young woman in the house brought me a glass of water, then sat close to me and shared that since this morning she had been feeling disturbed and oppressed in her spirit. Seeking release from this, she prayed and read her Bible but this feeling persisted.

However, the moment I stepped into their home, immediately whatever it was that was disturbing and oppressing her left, and she felt freedom and was at peace.

I replied and told her that when I came in, the Lord's presence came with me and where His presence is, there is liberty.

Nothing that is not of God can stand in His presence. I reminded her that as a child of God she too has the Holy Spirit and is also a carrier of God's presence. He goes with her everywhere and will work through her to change lives and even bring about miracles and healing as well as deliverance to those in bondage.

Many times, we do not fully realize the authority that is ours in Jesus. When we live and walk in intimate fellowship with God, we will see Him do wonders through us that will amaze us!

This communion with the Lord is available to ALL of us, for He is not a respecter of persons. Rich or poor, male or female, regardless of anything that others may say that disqualifies us, God desires to work in and through each of us, as His sanctified children. However, we must be fully dedicated, surrendered and set apart to live for Him, and be walking in the authority that is ours in Christ.

Heidi Baker says it well: "God has called His Bride to be carriers of His glory. To do this, we must deepen our life of sacrifice, prayer and abandoned love."

Chapter Nine

When I think of the supernatural healing the Lord did in Ashok's heart and life, it reminds me of the words of Fawn Parish in her book "It's All About You, Jesus," where she writes: "We must keep declaring the beauty and excellence of Jesus and leave the results to God. We are not responsible for the result of our obedience. We are not salvation detectives. Salvation belongs to the Lord. We are simply called to love and proclaim His Lordship."

I am thankful to God for the privilege of meeting dear Ashok and the grace that He gave me to show His love to him in such a tangible way.

I am also thankful for being able to introduce him to my precious Jesus, who will not only be his Saviour, but his Counselor and Guide and his best friend; the One who will never leave him or forsake him, regardless of whatever happens in his life.

The Lord not only allowed Ashok to experience His life-altering love and receive Him as his personal Saviour, but He also opened a wonderful door and blessed him with an excellent job abroad, where he currently resides.

Love this story by Fawn Parish: "International prayer leader David Bryant tells the story of how frustrated he once felt by being 'only' a prayer leader.

"Surely there were other kingdom advancing things he could be doing.

"One night about 2:00 AM David felt he heard the Lord say, 'Get the people to Me and I'll take them from there!' When Jesus is the at heart of our mentoring, we are doing just that—getting people to Jesus. We are teaching them to hear Jesus, to see Jesus in others, to find Jesus in the Word. The emphasis is more interactive than informative between Jesus and the one being mentored. Our goal is not to create clones of ourselves, but original followers of Christ."

This is exactly what I am called to do in my ministry: "Get the people to Jesus and He will take them from there."

I praise God for His heart of love for Ashok, whom He brought by way of His dear child, Becky, who had prayed for him and told him about me and my ministry. I rejoice in the joy that was mine to show him God's love that ultimately brought him to Jesus, who is the Way, the Truth, and the Life.

Only Jesus can bring about a total change in such a life as Ashok's, who had declared that he was beyond hope, and that God did not exist.

Chapter Nine

Do you want to be more like Jesus?

If so, then: "We must keep serving this broken world and keep on serving. God calls us not to an event, but to a lifestyle." wrote J. Daniel Lupton.

STOP FOR THE ONE

CHAPTER TEN

A Love That Shatters Addictions

Another story of God's great grace and deliverance is the story of a young man named Frank. He was a chain smoker and alcoholic. His parents were very troubled by his behavior. He would not listen to anyone and did as he wanted. He was arrogant, stubborn and was spending way too much time in the company of bad friends.

His parents were Catholic. They often implored the priest from their church to come and talk to him. Most times Frank would somehow sense their plans and he would run out of the house and be gone by the time the priest arrived. On the few times that he was still at home and someone would arrive to counsel him, he was very rude to them. He made it clear that he did not welcome them or need any help. It was his life and he would live it as he pleased.

I thank God for giving me the grace to be patient and continue to tirelessly love and reach out to the lost, lonely, hurting, unloved ones, and yes—also the addicted. Not everyone realizes that people who are addicted to something most times got into that state because of deep personal pain. Think about it. Nobody wants to be addicted. No one picks up that first drink or does their first drug in hopes of becoming dependent on them and losing control of their life. No! They are seeking a way of escape from the pain and welcome the few moments of liberation from what normally torments them.

When well-meaning people saw me associating with Frank and trying to understand and help him, they told me I was wasting my time. "A person like Frank is a hard-core alcoholic and he will not change!" Of course, I had already noticed Frank was tough and arrogant. It did not take their warning to get me to see that.

When dealing with a person who has high addiction or attitude issues, our constant intercession for them at the throne of grace is vitally important. Especially when they do not seem to change at all, or even have the desire to. Sometimes we view their condition as so irreparably damaged that real and lasting change seems almost hopeless.

Chapter Ten

But nothing is hopeless or impossible with God. Our "impossible" is nothing for God! Love never fails!

The addict's choice of how to live their life has been used by the enemy to not only destroy the person himself but countless other people who are associated with him in one form or another. The darkness that surrounds them is powerful and very real. I believe if we choose to be with them without being divinely compelled to become involved, that we can personally be harmed by their actions.

We must be divinely led to help others. The Spirit MUST be the one who does the leading, with our every move, step, word, or action.

All we must do is be the willing vessel that can be used for this purpose. We need never fear we will come up short in our assignment. If the Spirit of God brought Frank my way, then that same Spirit of God will fully equip me for the assignment.

I was one hundred percent confident that God had a big plan for Frank's life and future, which the enemy wanted very much to steal and destroy. We can have full assurance that our God is always victorious! He has come to set the captives free.

Yet the ultimate success may ride on just how willing we are to participate with Him in HIS plan. He wants us not just to work for Him but work WITH Him.

We have to remove ourselves from the equation along with our great ideas of what can be said or done to persuade people like Frank to leave their life of sin, and fully trust that GOD knows what will reach them more than we ever could. It's not easy!

Are we willing to pay the price to be merely an anonymous someone working behind the scenes while GOD gets all the glory?

The One who set me free has called me to be available to Him to be used in whatever way He desires. I do not wish to be known as anything but a servant of God who is known for my love.

Once a dear man of God told me that there is a young girl in their church who needed deliverance. He said many have prayed for her, but she had still not changed.

He requested if I could come some day and pray over her. He asked me if I have a deliverance ministry.

I replied, "I don't know about any deliverance ministry, but I do know that I have the DELIVERER in me!"

Chapter Ten

Immediately I began to think about how we are sometimes so quick to put labels on people. This person has a healing ministry. That person has a deliverance ministry.

Is this what we are supposed to be doing?

The disciples in the Bible were not proudly displaying their badges of healer, or deliverer. Yes, they DID heal and deliver countless people in terrible need, but it was in the Name of Jesus and for HIS glory only.

They did not wish to draw attention to themselves, for it was not anyone but God who did the actual healing and delivering, and they knew it. They were only His vessels, yielded and ready to be used by Him. We are called to pray for the sick and the ones who are bound, but it is Jesus and ONLY Jesus who does the healing and sets people free.

There is ALWAYS a reason why someone is turning to alcohol, or whatever other avenue they have chosen to deal with their pain. As we deal with the addict in love, our dear Lord will reveal the reasons behind the addiction and give us wisdom on how to proceed.

In Frank's life, I felt he was struggling from his relationship with his father, who was a very strict man.

STOP FOR THE ONE

He had received more than adequate instruction over the years, but not much love. I felt Frank needed a friend, someone who would not just give him guidance all the time but someone who would display God's heart of love for him and hold his hand through life.

So many mothers have spoken to me about problems with their children—could it be that the fathers were not present in their lives as the children needed them to be?

So many of our families are torn apart and hurt by absentee daddies! Some fathers were not there physically, others were in the house but rarely if ever were truly "there" for their children! The children then, in turn, rebel. They want to be loved equally by both their parents.

Nothing in a child's life can replace the love of a mother AND a father. These loves are different from each other, yet equally as vital! When this need is not satisfied, they sadly turn to whatever WILL be there for them.

My desire was to establish a friendly relationship with Frank. Until he was able to find me trustworthy, I knew he would not share his struggles with me. Nobody randomly pours out their heart to a stranger, for who is to say this stranger would not gossip or even mock the person for what was said?

Chapter Ten

Frank needed to know for sure that I would keep whatever he said between us only and would not look down upon him, for while he appeared tough and hardened outwardly, inside he was actually quite fragile. Without trust, we had nothing.

Again, I want to say that I did not want to preach to dear Frank.

All he needed was someone who would meet with him on a regular basis and spend quality time with him. Frank was touched as he realized he was worth spending time with.

If we want to see lives transformed, we should never attempt to win them over with our intellect. Progress takes time and the breakthrough we pray for will only happen if one has an honest and transparent relationship with the person and is not quick to tell them how things should be. I spent so much time with Frank, just to be with him.

I believe my job was to simply bring the love of the Father to Frank, not to tell him what to do or advise him in any other way. He longed for someone to just hear him and understand his feelings, right then. I did as I do with many—just listen, be understanding, sympathetic, and compassionate.

It was not easy dealing with Frank. He was a chain smoker and did not care that I was a "religious" man. He could not seem to go for more than a few moments after finishing his cigarette before lighting up another one. What does one do in a situation like this? I have learnt that when we minister to an addict, we need to accept them as they are.

I started meeting with Frank and we'd talk about whatever he wanted to talk about. He soon felt safe in my company because I would never try to advise, counsel, or preach to him, as he was used to everyone else doing. I would just spend time getting to know him. He was willing to see me and every so often I would stop by and spend some time with him or take him to a restaurant and talk over a cup of tea.

While sitting behind with me on my scooter, he would be smoking. I never told him not to smoke. I would just ignore it.

Sadly, a lot of people who noticed him sitting behind me on my scooter also noticed him smoking, and they began to spread the news that Brother Ravi's ministry is not biblical, since he allows the youth to smoke in his presence. The news spread like wildfire and fellow believers started talking about me, saying that I do not know how to properly counsel the youth.

Chapter Ten

Is there any surprise that so many young people today are turned off by the church, which can be so quick to judge? These youth need to know they are accepted "as is," without criticism or conditions. We must receive people as they are. This is not to say we accept their wrong choices. Sin is sin. However, we can still embrace the sinner.

There were times I was with Frank while he was drunk. Even in this state, he knew nothing but love from me, as we spent time together. In my ministry, it is absolutely vital to accept people as they are. It is so important the addict knows that love need not be conditional.

Chances are, a lot of the "love" they have experienced before, has been lacking.

I love the words by Clyde M. Narramore in his book entitled "Counselling Youth": "Through speech and through silence you can express this attitude of respect and esteem for your counselee. As you do, he can slowly begin to experience this acceptance of you and thereby develop a relationship in which you can help him."

God has taught me to love imperfect people, for I am also a member of that same group. He died for me while I was yet a sinner.

STOP FOR THE ONE

He loved me with all my imperfections. And today a lot of other imperfect people who are believers have begun to behave so high and mighty that they keep away from people who smoke and drink. We in our pride or self-righteous attitude would never want anyone to see us standing with someone who is smoking or drinking.

I remember reading somewhere, "When we love people, we must love what's good and accept what's still under construction."

Such truth in those words!

I will never forget when I first started going to church and had not yet found the Lord. I was smoking and drinking at that time. A dear family who was actively involved in their church used to invite me over to their home for dinner. Philip Uncle and Sheila Auntie always welcomed me and did their best to be sure I felt at home.

While I was spending time talking with them, I would light a cigarette. Instead of telling me not to smoke in their home, they would simply keep an ashtray in front of me. They were determined to love me as I was, and they spent our time together not scolding me but showing me the love of Jesus. They prayed for me, instead of giving me a sermon about smoking and drinking ruining my life.

Chapter Ten

Jesus sat and ate with sinners! Today? We, as men and women of God, have decided that we are so holy that we must distance ourselves from people who are smoking, drinking or into drugs. If you ask me, this is one of the biggest reasons why the church is so ineffective.

Do we value our "reputation" over the lives and souls of the broken, wounded, or wandering people? They are seeking answers, for something to soothe their pain. They need love, they need help—and the church is unwilling to accept them in their present condition? I believe a church is a hospital where we are to care for these dear ones and nurse them back to health.

My ministry's mission is to bind their wounds, apply balm to their bruises, and tenderly support each weak limb or heart until healing has taken place and they can go out and begin to reach others in the same way.

Don't get me wrong, I am not trying to cast dispersion upon the church or its believers. There are so many wonderful men and women of God who have been phenomenal in living their lives as Jesus did.

The world needs more of them! We need to have a burning desire to save the ones that are down and out and have been given up on by those who were supposed to love them the most.

STOP FOR THE ONE

Tell me please, if this desire is not within us; then what is the difference between the world and the church?

My ministry is not within the church walls, but out in the world. God has given me so much love to share with ALL people on the streets. I believe in speaking very little but SHOWING LOVE IN ACTION.

There are times when I am on my way back home late at night and I pause to minister to a person whom the Lord tells me to stop for. He may be drunk and in a very hopeless condition. I sit with him on the sidewalk and just listen to him, wipe his tears, and pray for him.

It frankly does not bother me if a believer sees me at such a late hour of the night sitting with an alcoholic on the sidewalk. It does not matter what they feel, think, or tell others.

The only thing that is of value to me is that I am obeying the Lord and doing what He has assigned me to do. I have come out of the "pleasing people zone" and am only conscious of the One I love.

I will go to any length to reach out and care for the ones He is burdened for and has sent my way.

Patrick Weaver once said: "Faith leaders are needed in the streets and at the table of social advocacy more so

Chapter Ten

than ever. Jesus did not stay in a box. Jesus took God to the streets. We cannot have effective inreach without effective outreach."

Knowing God as well as I do, I was able to discern that in only a few months, Frank would not only be set free from alcohol but would give his life to Jesus. My focus was on what I believed Jesus would do, so I was not concentrating on Frank's smoking and drinking. Instead, I shared with him how when I accepted Jesus, my intense desire for smoking died.

I had been a chain smoker as well, and I quit this habit because I fell so deeply in love with Jesus. I became consumed with knowing Him and walking with Him was so enjoyable that everything that was not of Him just faded away. I did not have to make any effort to stop. The Spirit of God did that awesome work for me!

I was never called to change Frank. We can change nobody, by ourselves. Only Jesus can do that! I was just called to love him and allow God to do the transformation.

I love this quote that I read somewhere: "One thing's for sure, God won't change the people we are trying to change; He has a 'hands off' policy. We must get out of His way and allow Him to work!"

STOP FOR THE ONE

The Spirit of God DID begin to work and minister in dear Frank's heart. He started attending the prayer meeting at my place on Saturdays!

The Lord knows how to perform that creative miracle we've been praying for, even in the most stubborn of hearts. We hand that loved one over to Him, and He does a perfect work! I know I am just an instrument to be used as He sees fit. On my own I am limited and ineffective. All I can ever do, I do by His grace after I have set aside my own ideas of how things need to proceed. His ways are so much higher than mine!

I was sure what God would do in Frank's situation would be so wondrous that everyone would behold the difference and be shocked at the radical change! Pure and simple, PRAYER would change Frank from the inside out and his attitude and actions would deeply reflect this new man that he would become.

Yes, Frank came to the place where he was convicted of all his sins. This is how the Holy Spirit works. He opens the eyes of those caught in sin, to see how grieved the heart of God is by their lifestyle. They begin to feel an incredible need to come clean and confess their sins so they can experience forgiveness and find that inner peace that the addictions they had never quite provided.

Chapter Ten

Frank wept and repented and gave his heart to Jesus. Not only did he receive the forgiveness of his sins but also astonishing deliverance from alcohol and smoking! He became a new creation in Christ Jesus, as the old things all passed away. (2 Corinthians 5:17)

He started reading the Bible and attending church with me on Sundays. His parents were so happy to see the change in their much-loved son, and they had great love and regard for me.

He began to grow in the grace and knowledge of Jesus Christ. One day he confided in me that he wanted to be baptized. My heart rejoiced upon hearing his desire to take the next step of faith and obedience! However, with this came a problem.

Frank said he wanted to be baptized without his parents' knowledge because they are Catholic, and they do not agree with baptism by immersion. I agreed to perform the ceremony in private. I informed a few close fellow believers and we had a wonderful time of celebration, with worship and God's Word. Frank obeyed the Lord in the waters of baptism. It was a NEW DAWN in his life. He no longer had the same look as he had before. He began to walk deeply in reverence of God. His love for Jesus and hunger and thirst for more of Him was very apparent to all.

One day shortly after that, as I was resting at home, I heard a loud knock on the door. It was Frank's father. Somehow, he had found out about Frank's baptism, and here he was, furious. He exploded in anger at me and as he was screaming, he told me I was to have no contact with Frank anymore.

I was NOT to meet with him ever again. I was quiet and allowed him to pour out his anger. After he finally stopped, I told him that becoming baptized in this way was Frank's desire and decision. No one had forced him into it. Frank had willingly come forward to obey the Lord in the waters of baptism. That did not seem to help much, so I told his dad that I will obey him and not meet with Frank.

Frank was very distressed when he heard that his dad had gone to see me. He knew his father was a very short-tempered man and he could guess what had been said. He was very concerned that there were things said in anger that had hurt me. Frank later confided that his dad had screamed at him as well, then strictly demanded he stay away from me.

Frank asked if we could meet without his father's knowledge. I told him no. He thought for a moment then asked if he could call me. I agreed to that idea but said again that we must not meet face to face.

Chapter Ten

I told Frank that he needed to show his family through his life, actions, behaviour and especially his reactions, that he is a changed person. I told him to let his family see that not only has he been delivered from alcohol and smoking but his heart had also changed.

He needed to obey his dad and not meet me. I asked him to pray for his parents and not react angrily if they shouted at him again, but let his reaction be Christ-like. I assured him of my prayers for him and told him that I had no doubt that one day his father would call me and ask me to please come back to visit. God would work wonders, but we needed to pray and wait for HIS timing. In HIS time, He makes all things beautiful.

I asked him, in the meantime, to take a stand for the Lord and His Word and go to the Bible believing church that we had talked about before. He started attending church every Sunday.

I kept praying hard for dear Frank and especially also for his parents. It is one thing to bring a soul to the saving knowledge of the Lord but quite another to guide and counsel him after that decision!

I wanted Frank to stand for the One he had embraced, and continue to draw ever closer to Him while learning to depend upon Him more and more.

STOP FOR THE ONE

I told him during one of our phone calls that I missed him terribly, but honoring his parents was so very important.

I've heard of people who have come to know the Lord and they shared their decision with their family that they were saved, yet they were still terribly disobedient to their parents. If we are truly saved, it would show through our life!

The Bible clearly states that we are to honor our parents and care for them!

One story that illustrates this comes to mind. A man from a Syrian Orthodox church told me once that after his son accepted the Lord Jesus that he quickly made several important decisions. One was to leave the church his father attended.

The man understood the reason for his leaving the church, but what he did not understand was that his son also said he was leaving his profession to serve the Lord.

This man and his wife had spent all of their money to put their son through the necessary schooling to become a doctor, and now he wanted to leave it all behind?

Chapter Ten

The parents were up in years by this time, and the father sadly asked if this is the way the Lord works—first to take their son away, then leave them wondering how they will be able to make ends meet! I told him I would speak to his son.

I called this man and we spoke for a while. He told me that his new pastor was saying the son had a calling to serve the Lord full time, so he should leave his profession and join the pastor in the church. I asked him if he himself had heard from God clearly in this matter, and he replied that he had not.

I told him that he has a responsibility to take care of his parents, especially since they had given all they had to him, for him to get his medical degree. How would he feel if his parents now lost their home because they had nothing left? Until he personally hears from the Lord to give up his job and serve Him full time, he should continue what God assigned for him to do.

This also can be a calling!

He saw the wisdom behind these words, took a job in a hospital, and cared for his parents. It is incredibly important to wisely and prayerfully guide young believers to be sure they stay on the course God set for them.

STOP FOR THE ONE

I continued to intercede in prayer for dear Frank and his parents. Only a few months after his father angrily confronted me at my home, his parents could not deny the transformation in their son. They called and requested I please come to their home. I visited them and Frank's dad asked me for forgiveness for his words spoken harshly in anger.

We had a wonderful time of fellowship and prayer. The family experienced blessing upon blessing as his parents and younger brother also gave their lives to Jesus and were baptized!

Oh, the joy that the filled Frank that day!

What a confirmation of God's provision in his life! Our God touched one person, Frank, and through his changed life, the whole family gave their hearts to Jesus. I have seen it over and over that when we believe and leave our loved ones in God's hands; as we pray and wait, He will amaze us.

Frank's dad began to invite his friends and relatives to his home, and he asked me to share the love of Jesus with them. Between hearing about God and seeing the "new" Frank, some of those who came had their eyes opened, and they accepted the truth of the Bible and started following the Lord!

Chapter Ten

Does the story end here? No! Praise God for not only did He deliver Frank from his past life as an alcoholic, He completely transformed his life as Frank learnt to die daily to himself and be alive to Him, His will, His plan and purposes.

The Lord in His mercy and goodness called dear Frank to serve him! Frank answered the call, obeyed the Lord, and today, Frank is the pastor of a church. Look what the Lord has done!

If I had become embarrassed about all the people who were talking about me when Frank was smoking while on the back of my scooter or while I was sitting and talking with him in public as he was intoxicated, I would have started to avoid him, to save my "reputation."

Tragically, this is the way the Church can miss out on those dear people that God brings our way. We become people conscious, and do not want to take the risk of being opposed and misunderstood by others.

We are more concerned about not tarnishing our good name or our enviable position in Church, than we are for the souls that are lost and wandering, with no one to care for them or share the love of Jesus with. How this must make our Father's heart ache!

STOP FOR THE ONE

I will say it again. Frank did not change overnight. How did the change come? It came slowly and for that there was a price to pay, to see Frank with the eyes of Jesus. How could I not care for this young man when I remembered that Jesus saw me in the condition that I was in, which was much like Frank's.

Jesus did not turn away. He died for me! Yes, he gave His life for me, before I ever loved him, before I acknowledged my need for Him, while I was still a sinner!

He gave me the grace to lay down many things for Frank's sake, whom the Lord loved so deeply. I had to take time to recharge myself with my Lord. I had to be patient and willing to listen even when I knew there was much "I" could say.

Sitting with an alcoholic can take a lot out of you, yet even in his inebriated state Frank remembered and was touched by my willingness to be there with him. Yes, it took a lot of prayers to get through to dear Frank. And today, the Lord is using His servant Frank to reach out to many others. That's how it should be.

God used a mentor to reach me. He used me to touch Frank. And now Frank is helping others, who will in turn point even more people to the Lord!

Chapter Ten

Let me close with these words in Michele Perry's book "Love Has A Face": "A movement of love is arising in those who will choose to lay down their lives each day, becoming the expression of God's grace and goodness to the people He brings them. Still the prayer I had prayed nearly every day for over a decade remained: Jesus, let me love with Your love and see with Your eyes. Show me what it means to be the expression of Your heart to those around me. Because I knew more than ever that His love did indeed have a face: mine."

STOP FOR THE ONE

CHAPTER ELEVEN

Love, off the Clock

As a child of God, we can rest assured that our Lord delights in setting up divine appointments between someone who is hurting and in desperate need of encouragement and His child who will obediently reach out to that person, just listen for a while, then share God's heart without judgment.

One such example of a meeting planned by God happened several years ago, when He decided to allow a man named Moses and I to cross paths, right on time when it was most needed. God already knew and pre-planned for me to be driving down the road for a house meeting where I was to share the Word, just as Moses was arriving at the same intersection at the exact same time.

I love to be used by Him like this, in the ways that He chooses to use me for a specific person's needs at a very specific time! I was stopped at the crossing and as I waited for a chance to move again, I took notice of a man driving towards me on a motorcycle.

It was Moses. He was excited upon seeing me, and he stopped his motorcycle and took me aside.

We knew each other. We had met previously. He said, "Brother, God knew what my family and I were going through, and it is He who has brought us together here."

Moses was deeply hurting, both emotionally and mentally. He wept, sharing his heartbreaking situation. Moses had begun to feel that God did not love him and his family anymore because of the intense trials they had been going through, and they were still fighting these trials without seeing any relief. He desperately needed encouragement and prayer.

I am so glad that Moses realized that God had cared about him enough to send me, His servant, to care for him and to love and encourage him at the precise moment during that very difficult time when he most needed to hear that he was not forgotten or cast away by God.

He was hurting and needed to see and encounter God in a new way, right then. And, here I was, led by the Holy Spirit to show him that God had indeed not forgotten him and that He still cared deeply for him. Isn't it wonderful that our God is always an on-time God, sending help right as it is most needed?

Chapter Eleven

I've heard it said that, "If you want to follow Jesus, you'll have to open your heart to a cry that nobody else is listening to. You've got to listen to the Spirit within you. He'll tell you where to go, and He'll tell you whom to minister to."

This is exactly how we are to respond with the heart of God towards people: to meet them where they are, and where they are hurting, even if it is only just a shoulder upon which they can cry or lean on.

This is the ministry God has given me. It is not with eloquent words or long speeches that we will change hearts, but it is the love of God within us that will heal the broken-hearted no matter how deep the wounds.

Yes, I had been on my way to a meeting and I was to be the speaker, but here was a man who was in deep need at that same moment. I had to put everything on hold in order to minister to this person who so desperately needed help. To God as well as to me, Moses was important, and I needed to adjust my plans—no matter how well prepared—and show that I sincerely cared. Everything else could wait. I needed to keep this divine appointment between Moses and myself, and just sit and listen to his heart cry and allow him to share his deep pain and hurt.

STOP FOR THE ONE

I would not tell him that I had only 15 minutes before I was to be at this important meeting and that there were people waiting for me.

I understood that even more important than sharing a message in that meeting was this man in a situation who needed all of me, including my time, my undivided attention, and my tender loving care.

While being at that meeting was something God approved of, I was called instead to be a living testimony to a hurting man and spend that time with him. The meeting could go on without me, but Moses had no one else. I could ignore this man, then go and share a sermon in the meeting.

My heart goes out to the hurting and broken, and I always look for ways to help them. Those who are discouraged, depressed, and down and out have a special place in my heart, for I remember the times I have been deeply hurt myself, and I know what it feels like. It is easy to say we care about a person then say a hasty prayer and walk away without really helping them. We need to show that we truly care by casting aside our own agenda. I stopped for the one God sent my way, knowing it would mean the meeting would be affected. Moses became my priority. He deeply needed me right at that divinely set-up moment!

Chapter Eleven

I read somewhere and it is so true that, "Compassion will rearrange your priorities! The Good Samaritan decided that where he was going wasn't as important as where he was at that particular moment."

I love the words of Michele Perry: "When many others turn away, Jesus turns my eyes to see what He sees. It is in the seeing that makes one stop. Jesus spoke of another man, the Good Samaritan, who chose to stop. The account of the Good Samaritan challenges me that I have not truly seen until I am willing to stop. It is a reminder that I will never be able to become an accurate expression of Love's heart until I learn to see through Love's eyes. This Samaritan risked his life to help the traveler. He bandaged his wounds. He gave him water to drink. He put clothes on his beaten body. He took him to an inn where the traveler could recover. What a beautiful story of love Jesus told in the parable of the Good Samaritan! Jesus was always pushing the envelope to make a point. So, who was the face of His love? Was it the face of religion? Was it the face of devotion? Was it the face of title or position? Was it a face of success? No. It was a face of an unknown stranger who had eyes to see the one in need and loved enough to stop."

STOP FOR THE ONE

I called those I was to be with in the house meeting and told them I would not be able to attend. I informed them that the Lord had brought someone my way who needed help immediately, then I asked them to just go ahead and spend time in worship and prayer.

There is a wonderful quote about the Good Samaritan from the devotional "Word for Today" by Bob Gass: "When a mugging victim was left for dead on the Jericho Road, a priest and a Levite both 'passed by on the other side.' But what if they overlooked the man not because they lacked compassion, but because they were late for a Bible study or a prayer meeting? Would they have been justified?"

One pastor said, "This parable didn't register until I'd been in ministry for years. I'd walked past so many people who could've used my help, but because I was too distracted by church activities, broken lives by the roadside rarely fit into my agenda. Love isn't efficient, and it can't be scheduled. This hurting man couldn't have waited three weeks for an appointment, or for the Samaritan to launch a ministry to care for similar victims."

Bob Gass went on further: "Three people in this story were given a chance to help a dying man lying by the side of the road. Only one took it—the other two were

Chapter Eleven

too busy and missed it. We tend to think that if God's going to use us, it'll be after we've been to seminary, fasted and prayed. I've been to seminary, fasted and prayed, analyzed every angle, weighed the pros and cons and have all my ducks in a row. No! Opportunities are coming at you every day. The question is, will you act on them or let them pass you by?"

I believe many times that the greatest gift of caring we can give to someone in need is the gift of our presence. Not that we attempt to explain away their pain but to just be with them in it. When people are so deep in pain and agony, they need someone to come alongside them to show them the Lord's love and compassion.

There are a lot of wandering people feeling sad, hopeless, empty, hurting, wounded and lonely. There are divine appointments all around us!

Will we accept them?

I'm so overjoyed to have my heart so filled with His love that I sincerely love to go out and find people in need and be His love and encouragement to them. That is what Jesus would do too if He walked the earth right now. People need real love and encouragement. And we can be just that—an instrument of God's love to a hurting world!

STOP FOR THE ONE

Ron Hembree makes a very good point in his book "The Speck in Your Brother's Eye": "It is a strange paradox but nevertheless true that our very dedication to reach the lost makes us ignore people in the deepest need. Surely this is one of the main points Jesus makes in the dramatic parable of the Good Samaritan. The priest and the Levite were so preoccupied with their religious responsibilities they had no time to see the broken and battered man by the road."

Are you too busy to care about the needs of others? Are you so engrossed in your religious activities that you're missing life-or-death opportunities right in front of you?

I didn't stop with just listening to Moses and counseling him.

I needed to allow the Holy Spirit to minister healing into his hurting heart. What if Moses had not had the opportunity to share the burdens in his heart? All that he was going through could have overwhelmed him to the point where he gave up. But look at how Jesus with His love for all of us, brought Moses to me—literally face-to-face on our motorcycles at a red light at an intersection! God is mindful of all those who are hurting.

Chapter Eleven

He sees their tears, knows their struggles, and will custom pick one of His available, yielded children to go and minister to that one in pain.

J. Daniel Lupton in his book, "I Like Church, But… " says: "Caring means commitment, and, for many people, time is more important than money. Even the simplest acts of caring require time. A conversation that would bless a friend's life may go unspoken because of the rush from church to home for a football game. Jesus tells the story of the robbed and beaten man who was ignored by two passersby before a Samaritan took time to come to his aid [see Luke 10:30-35]. It may be that those who passed him didn't feel any sympathetic nudging to help, or it may be they wanted to care, but their next appointment was too pressing to allow them to stop. Don't let that become your excuse. If you want to be cared for, you must take the time to care for others."

What I said to Moses as simply as possible was that God certainly does love him. I told him that what was happening in his life must be given to the Lord. It is certainly unfortunate that a humble and sincere person like him should go through what he went through.

I reminded him that despite his family asking him to see a doctor and take medication for the deep depression he suffered with so badly for so long, that he had overcome and gone four years was a miracle by itself!

I had advised him not to see the doctor for those mind altering drugs because he believed in the Word of God and in the power of prayer and was open to counseling. The Lord supernaturally and miraculously did heal and deliver him from this condition! I counseled him to take each day as it comes, as a blessing from God. I reminded him that whatever his problems might be on the home front to please not give up. Keep hoping in the only One who can and will bring comfort to him in one way or another.

I shared with him that I too had been through many fierce trials, tears, persecutions and challenges, but I had seen and experienced one thing all through my life: even in my darkest moments, when everyone else had abandoned me, never for a moment throughout all my days did God leave me.

He is the Only One who is constant. He is unchanging. People are here today and gone tomorrow. They can be very close to you in one moment and then the next moment they leave you. They can lift you and then drop you, but God is everlastingly the same. Always the same yesterday, today and forever. His constant presence, love, and care have always been there.

He has stood with me and loved me in the most critical times when I otherwise would have found myself alone and forsaken by all.

I once heard that, "Often when God puts you close to someone and makes you privy to certain information, He does it so that you can speak a word in season to him who is weary. [Isaiah 50:4]" I got close enough to know Moses' real problem, then introduced him to the One who had the solution.

That's what Jesus did! Listen! *"And seeing the multitudes, He felt compassion for them, because they were distressed and downcast."*[Matthew 9:36]

I took a lot of time to physically be with dear Moses, and pray for him, without rushing him or watching the clock. The Lord strengthened and comforted him. We parted that day after I assured him of my prayers, and I also told him that I would visit his family the next day.

And visit them, I did! I spent much time with his family. This precious family was touched by the love of God that they received through me, God's servant. The same God who knows our weaknesses and our hurts comforted this hurting family and showed Himself strong on their behalf!

He provided healing, deliverance and worked wonders and miracles in this family, much more than we could think, ask or imagine!

Not only did God bring Moses and his family out of their critical problem, but He also settled the wedding of Moses' son and daughter, and today, this whole family stands as a testimony to God's glory.

If anyone... sees his brother in need but has no pity on him, how can the love of God be in him? (1 John 3:17)

Tim Hansel tells of a seminary professor who had an unusual way of making his point in class. His students were to study, put into practice, then preach on The Good Samaritan.

The campus was large, and the luckier students had ten minutes between classes, while others had less time, which forced them to rush in order to get to each class on time. Each of the students had to walk down a certain corridor and pass by a "beggar" who had been deliberately planted there by the professor.

What happened was a powerful lesson! The number of would-be preachers who stopped to help this man was extremely low, especially those who were under the pressure of getting to their next class on time!

STOP FOR THE ONE

Rushing to preach their sermon on The Samaritan, most walked right past the beggar heart of the parable!

This is the ministry God has called me to. To lo the one. To be there for the one. To help the o write to the one. To speak of God's amazing gra gift of salvation to the one. Jesus left the crowd to heal and minister to the one, because one life is wo much to God. One soul is worth saving. One li it took to keep Jesus on the cross.

It is time for all of us to boldly obey the Spirit, in fre and in love for Him and His needy ones, and t "seeing" the needs of those around us. We must love in action!

CHAPTER TWELVE

Love STOPS!

When I am riding the streets on my bike, my eyes keep looking to and fro, gazing at the faces of people in their cars, on their bicycles or walking on the roadside and I just say a prayer, "Lord, I wonder what these people are going through, how many know You? What are the hurts and wounds they carry in their heart? I wonder if they have anyone to share their inner pain?" I feel for them and just say a prayer, "Lord, touch and bless each one that I am passing by. Reveal Your love and bring peace and healing into their heart."

One evening as I was riding my bike down one of the streets and it was kind of dark. Suddenly my gaze fixed on one man who was walking on the footpath. I noticed that he was walking very slowly and his hand was on his chest.

Immediately I STOPPED and asked him if he was well. He looked at me and asked if he knew me and if we had met earlier.

I told him no, we had not met earlier, but it was the Spirit of God that caused me spot him in the crowd and He asked me to stop and inquire about you. Tears flowed down his face as he said, "God is so concerned about me, that He made you notice me and stop for me?"

I told him that my ministry is to *Stop for the One*. He leads me to and to hug them with His love! I love to be available to Him so when He looks down from heaven to us here on earth, that He won't say, "I looked for one to be My heart, and I found none."

He will find me because I am available to Him 24/7! He has always been there for me and now He can count on me being there for Him. It is up to Him to show me whom to reach out to and care for. I will be ready and willing because we are the vessels through whom He can reach out to those who need a touch from Him the most. There are so many needs that people have and it's sad that He is not able to find more people who are WILLING and READY to REACH OUT and CARE for others.

How true are the words I read somewhere, "Seeing people through God's eyes causes them to be attracted and open to you."

Chapter Twelve

Pratap stood still and with tears in his eyes, he shared that he had just finished work at his job and he was walking to take a bus home when he suddenly started having chest pain and was finding it difficult to walk.

He was wondering how he would make it home, worried that it could be a heart problem because he had high blood pressure. I told him that he would be fine because the God who led me to him in the midst of so many people was very concerned about him and He would touch and heal him. I told him that I was going to pray for him and he would be absolutely fine. He smiled, and here I was in the crowded area, laying my hands on Pratap and praying over him.

I spoke healing in Jesus' name into his body and the Spirit of God immediately touched and healed him. After prayer I asked him how he was feeling and he said he had NO PAIN and he felt peace flowing over him. He was so thankful and with tears flowing, he kept thanking me. I told him to thank the Lord Jesus, who cares so deeply for him, because I am only a vessel available that He could use for His glory.

Now to meet a stranger on the road and be willing to pray over them then and there—THAT is what taking the church to the streets looks like. Our faith is meant to spill out of the building we have church in and out into

STOP FOR THE ONE

the streets where it is needed the most. God is God in the church and outside the church! He is God at the grocery store and gas station. He is God in restaurants and our workplaces. He is simply waiting for us to realize it and agree with Him for miracles everywhere we go!

I love the words of dear Heidi Baker, from her book, 'Compelled by Love', "A minister's job is not simply to preach on a platform, standing up in front of a crowd of people while a big film crew records the service. This is not our primary purpose. Our job is to love each person, one at a time, to stop and lend help every day for each of the suffering and the sick. Some of you may think ministry is a grand adventure. Ministry, however, is simply about loving the person in front of you. It's about stopping for the one and being the very fragrance of Jesus to a lost and dying world."

My ministry is all about carrying HIM— HIS PRESENCE— to where people are and letting Him minister to them, then and there. Yes, the church should go to the streets and demonstrate His love and power for all to see HIM and be in awe of Him.

Would you go up to a complete stranger that the Lord leads you to on the street and say, "Do you have any problem that I can pray with you for?" Or you would just leave a tract with someone and walk away?

Chapter Twelve

I LOVE praying for people ... any place ... anywhere ... and at any time! I am not self-conscious of people around who watch me—all I am conscious about is there is so much need around us and we need to be His hands and His feet, carrying and being His love to the ones in need.

There are countless people around us who are sad, hopeless, empty, lonely and hurting—in need of someone to reach out to them and love them. There are divine appointments all around us, if we would only see and accept them.

How true are these words by Roch D. from his book, 'The Price of the Anointing', "God releases the COMPASSION ANOINTING through the lives and ministry of those who will pay the price of cultivating a sensitive heart. It is only with a sensitive heart that we can truly identify with the needs of His people. God expects us to be caring enough to step out of our comfort zones and reach out in love."

I heard this somewhere, "True ministry is being able to hear the cry of the wounded heart and minister the heart of God to them!"

I asked Pratap to sit on my vehicle so I could drop him off at home and he was taken aback by my offer!

Instead, he said it would be fine if I could just drop him off at the bus stop. But I insisted that I would drop him off at his house! Pratap sat with me and though his house was quite a distance away, it's always my joy to go the distance for Him.

It's all about obeying and pleasing HIM, so distance doesn't matter because the person matters so much more. Oh, that's the love of God!

I love the words of Emilie Barnes who said, "CARING is another form of service. I serve God and others when I notice their needs and act in ways that will help them."

On the way home, Pratap opened his heart and shared how he was hurting—how he had lost his job because the factory he was working in closed down. He had taken a part time job because he needed to take care of his children and their education. He shared with me about his family. I was so glad I could take him home and more than that, I was happy to meet his family!

I sensed that the Lord had BIG plans in connecting us! It didn't stop by just praying for him on the road and he was healed. God's eyes and heart were on Pratap and his family and He wanted to accomplish His purposes for them. It was my joy to meet his wife and children. I had a cup of tea with them and prayed for them.

Chapter Twelve

But the association with Pratap did not end there! I continued to meet him often at his work place and spend time with him.

He felt God's love through me and he knew I CARED so he knew he could open up and unburden his heart. He shared his hurt and pain and expressed that he was now at peace because God had sent me to be by his side to pray, to care, and to be there for him and his family.

He became close to me, he would look forward to my visit with him, and he also invited me to his house for prayers. I would visit his place and pray and share God's Word. Through the power of God's love, the family came to the saving knowledge of Jesus Christ and received many untold blessings!!

Pratap, his wife and children love the Lord deeply! The Lord blessed his children and they are well settled. God did something REMARKABLE in the life and family of Pratap … all because I had God's grace to be available to Him, to be obedient to STOP and minister His love to Pratap. The Lord had Pratap and his family on His heart and I am so grateful I could be HIS love to them.

BEING God's love is more powerful than preaching. As Heidi Baker often says, "Just love the person in front of you." It's simple but profound!!!

J.Daniel Lupton said in his book, 'I Like Church, But...' "Jesus specialized in helping and healing the wounded. He had the wonderful ability to look at a sea of faces and see individuals needing His love."

People are so in need of LOVE—simply LOVE them!

How important it is to CARE! BE HIS LOVE AND ENCOURAGEMENT to the ones in need. I love to go out to the streets to search for and find the wounded ones I am led to, then love and encourage them.

Sometimes I bring them home until the Lord makes them whole again.

Heidi Baker said in the same book, "A minister is simply a sent one. You might only be sent across the street, but it does not matter. To God, whether it is to the one or the masses, it is the same— it is love incarnate."

I love the words of a dear friend, Jeff Symons, "The testimony of my life will be love. I will forever be known as a radical lover of God and of those He brings into my life."

I would like to close with these words by Michele Perry from her book, 'Love has a Face', "Love is learning the names of the nameless, seeing and stopping for the one in front of me until that person becomes so transformed by love that he or she will stop for the one in front of him or her. In this way perhaps a city, a region, a nation will be transformed by love, one life at a time."

STOP FOR THE ONE

CHAPTER THIRTEEN

Love Sees When Others Turn Away

Many years back, God led me to meet a precious elderly brother, Abraham. He loved God and had great love for the servants of the Lord that came into his life.

It did not take much time after we first met for the Spirit of God to bring us into a wonderful enduring friendship of mutual respect and honor. His prayers for me and my ministry were a great blessing to me. He was a man of prayer and asked me to join him at his home once a week for a time of fellowship and prayer. I told him I would do so, and began to visit his house.

Every time I arrived, I was eagerly welcomed. Abraham, his wife, daughter-in-law and the grandchildren would gather around as I shared the Word and prayed for them. I soon noticed however that his son, who most times was in the house but in another room, would not come in to join us.

I did not ask Abraham anything about his son but instead would just quietly pray for him. During one of the weekly visits, dear Abraham shared his burden with me. His son, Luke, did not join them for their family prayer time just as he was not joining when I visited them.

Abraham confided that this was because his son had been hurt by the church and Christians, so Luke had stopped going to church and reading his Bible. I told him that I will keep his son in prayer. My heart went out to Luke. I sensed he was lost in his own loneliness and thought no one would understand the pain he was going through, or be willing to really reach out to listen and care.

From that day on, whenever I visited Abraham's house, while in prayer, I would pray for Luke out loud, using words of encouragement: "Jesus You love Luke with an everlasting love and he is precious to You. He is the apple of Your eye and may You bless him abundantly."

This went on for a few weeks, but Luke still did not come to join us. Once, Abraham asked if he should call his son out to meet me. I told him to just let him be. Whenever Luke felt ready or desired from his heart to see me, he would come on his own.

Chapter Thirteen

I knew God was working behind the scenes, and I did not want to push myself or compel Luke to do something he may not have been ready for. Even though Luke and I never saw each other face-to-face in these meetings, I knew with God's guidance that the right words when used with love have the power to change the most stubborn hearts—even those listening from another room.

So, I kept visiting and naming him in prayer, knowing he was nearby, hearing what I was saying. Once, while the family and I were discussing food, I mentioned to Abraham that I love Andhra food—a delicious, very regional preparation from the Andhra Pradesh state in southern India. I am particularly fond of the non-veg dishes.

The following week, after prayer, Luke's wife invited me for lunch. I told her that I could not confirm if I could come quite yet, but would let her know. She replied that her husband, Luke, had asked her to invite me! He had overheard me sharing the other day that I love Andhra food, and Luke and family are from Andhra so they are very familiar with preparing that food.

I knew for sure then that Luke had been listening to our conversations and had heard all I had shared and said in prayer. I told her that if Luke had invited me, then I will surely come. I came the following week and after prayer, joined them for lunch. It was delicious! I asked Abraham's daughter-in-law to convey my thanks to dear Luke for the honor of being invited for lunch, and that I thoroughly enjoyed the food. I felt that the timing was still not right to rush to talk to Luke in person, since he did not come out to meet me, himself. It's so important to give people space and not be in a hurry to barge in or intrude, and end up making a mess of things. If we instead just wait and trust and allow God to move, He always does amazing work.

It is so important to be led by the Lord and be wise when we minister to people. There are so many different problems and divergent personalities. I could relate to Luke and understand his temperament, for I too was very shy and reserved in my earlier years. Luke had been deeply hurt by the church, as I said before, and had no desire to meet another Christian who might only add to that pain. It reminded me of Mahatma Gandhi, who said, "I love Jesus but I do not like Christians."

We can turn people off by rushing into things, and because of that they turn away from God. Someone once said that there are four gospels. You and I are the fifth gospel. What are people reading from your life and my life?

Chapter Thirteen

Are they able to SEE Christ in us, or is there no difference between us and the people of the world?

I could have told Abraham to tell Luke to come out while we were having our time of fellowship. I could have given Luke a sermon, saying he should look to Jesus and not people, since people will fail and hurt him but Jesus never would.

I could have counseled him and told him to read his Bible and be part of the family prayer time again. He may have done so, but would it have been done only to please me, and not because he desired to do so from his heart?

Again, I needed God's wisdom there as to how to delicately, wisely and tenderly deal with Luke. Another sermon would not help—he's heard plenty of them. Counseling sessions would also not do much good, for he has had a lot of those as well, and was still completely closed off to meeting with any Christians or having anything to do with church. He had moved away from Jesus.

And who was responsible for that? We, the men and women of God! The fault lies in us. We lacked love. Real, true, unconditional love as we have been loved by God—LOVE.

We may have outstanding knowledge of our religion but miss out on the most important part of living the Christian life, and that is living a life full of LOVE.

We act out of our human understanding and wisdom but forget to add the "heart" equation where "head" knowledge will only fail, much like the Pharisees in the Bible.

They were willing to tell others very quickly what they were doing wrong from their high spiritual pedestals, yet they did not feel compassion for them or put themselves into other people's shoes before passing judgement.

There are many people that have been wounded and experienced hurts and disappointments in the church. If we are open and honest with ourselves and are able to discern what God is showing us and be willing to hear what God is speaking to us, we can fall on His grace to correct our mindset and bring about real change in how we minister to others.

Someone once said: "What is wrong with the world? The reply was—I am wrong with the world!" I would like to change that to "What is wrong with the church? The reply should be—I am wrong with the church! Change has to start with me."

Chapter Thirteen

Luke had become so bitter that he had built a wall to protect himself from further pain, and he secluded himself behind it and would not allow anyone to disturb him there. I honestly believe that walls like this can only be breached by the LOVE of GOD.

Ron Hembree once said: "What if we can help our grieving and hurting brothers and sisters through this horrible night and gently walk with them up the long slopes of sorrow until they find themselves in the pure light of acceptance and warmth? The answer is not for the hurting to leave the Church but for the Church to come to them in their sorrow."

Put another way, by Kathy Troccoli: "When we're really honest with ourselves we have to admit that there are often times when we fail to love, when we fail to care about those around us."

Luke sensed something different in me, without seeing my face, without actually meeting me. He sensed that I sincerely LOVE others and I am different. No, it is not "ME" that broke down the walls around Luke, but CHRIST in me.

I understood where he came from because I, too, have been hurt by people who gave me lots of sermons and counseling instead of attempting to understand me and show me love. They felt they could judge me rather than accept me as I was, treat me with His love, and deal with me by His wisdom.

So now, when I look back and remember how it felt to be treated this way, I thank God for ALL that I went through and learnt. My own painful experiences made me sensitive to those who need to be handled tenderly and delicately, and my wish is to never repeat the same mistakes myself that others made when dealing with me.

I pray before every word I speak and move I make. I have learnt from others' mistakes and gained insight and patience. I understand just how easy it would have been to become bitter when treated like this, but with God's help and by His grace alone it made me a better, stronger and wiser person. Be encouraged!

None of the experiences we go through are wasted because God uses them for our good and His glory.

Without meeting dear Luke face-to-face, God had put His love in my heart for him.

Augustine once said: "What does love look like? It has the hands to help others. It has the feet to hasten to the poor and needy. It has eyes to see misery and want. It has

Chapter Thirteen

the ears to hear the sighs and sorrows of men. That is what love looks like."

We are called to be carriers of His divine love. I love the words of Heidi Baker: "God has spoken to me many times that my job is to love and His job is to heal."

It was easier for me to criticize Luke and agree with his father that he had backslid, God was displeased with him, and he needed to repent and return back to God, like the prodigal son. But I felt that Luke had not backslidden as much as the pastors and evangelists had missed out on showing him love and handling him with God's care and wisdom.

We, the men and women of God, are the ones who need to repent and return to God! We have become controlling, judgmental and critical—giving up on people if they do not respond to our efforts in our way, in our time—and they leave and go away. Even more sad is that after this we do not have any burden to go and bring them back.

We just really don't care.

One day, I could not contain my joy. I visited dear brother Abraham's house, and Luke came out of his room to greet me! Glory to God!

Luke sat with us for some time. What did I do that pulled him out of his den? What caused him to have the courage to come out of seclusion?

If it was just to see another Christian, he would have never ventured out. It was only because he was attracted to the genuine love of Christ that was flowing through me from heaven to his heart, through my prayers.

He also was given complete freedom to have his own space, and all the time he needed to come out on his own to meet me. It was such a good time talking with him and everyone was overjoyed when he was there during the prayer time as well. I love the way God works!

We so easily could dismiss people like Luke when they shut themselves off and stop coming to church, reading the Bible or being part of the family prayer time. We label them as backslidden but forget to notice the deep hurt and pain they carry. Sadly, no one cares, no one makes the sacrifice to see or help the person come out of their shell and experience God's deep healing.

This day with Luke was just the beginning! After that, whenever I visited Abraham, Luke met with me as well and there even came a time when he felt completely comfortable with me and began to open up and share on a much more personal level.

Chapter Thirteen

Praise God for the way His love brought healing to the long-standing wounds that dear Luke had been carrying around for so long.

Eventually, he went back to reading his Bible and praying on his own, because he fell in love with the Lord! He said that it was God who brought me to him. Had I not come, he would have gone deeper into his shell. It was already affecting his family. Now the relationship was mended and he and his family were happy. Luke was a transformed person because LOVE REACHED OUT TO HIM AND HEALED HIM.

We must humble ourselves and go in search of those who are hurting, to bring them back to Abba Father. Dwight L. Moody said: "If we have got the true love of God shed abroad in our hearts, we will show it in our lives. We will not have to go up and down the earth proclaiming it. We will show it in everything we say or do."

I would like to end this story with the words of Kenneth C. Haugk: "Christians are responsible for care; God is responsible for cure.

Caring for another person involves meeting the needs of that whole person. Through actions of love, God reaches down and touches people with his power. My caring provides a channel through which God's love can flow. My words and actions of love concretely demonstrate the good news.

The work of evangelism-caring/caring-evangelism cannot be accomplished if I restrict myself to my ecclesiastical ghetto, or if I speak the gospel without being the gospel. I need to get out into the world where people desperately need the love of Jesus Christ. So do you. May the Lord enable us to get on with the task at hand."

CHAPTER FOURTEEN

Love Pays Attention

A few years ago the Lord impressed upon me that He had been burdened for two men. He brought these men my way and made it clear that I was to pray for them and show them His love.

Those two people were Rajan and Vijay. Both were very troubled, hurt and broken by how life had turned out. Shortly after meeting Rajan and Vijay, the Lord placed a strong burden in my heart for them, and I began to pray intensely for both of them. I knew they were hurting. I needed to pay some attention to them.

Vijay was a follower of Jesus Christ, but was discouraged and felt he had no one whom he could trust enough to fully open his heart and share his struggles with. So many believers are going through deep hidden conflict. They are unable to find help either because they truly have no one to confide in, or feel as though they could never trust anyone enough to share their deep inner struggle with.

They put up a front that says all is well, and no one seems to figure out what is under their facade or care to notice the pain within. I believe that people occasionally don't need a pastor or counselor. Sometimes, they just need a devoted friend.

I felt dear Vijay had missed out on having a friend whom He could feel safe to share his anguish with. I am so humbled that God gave me His eyes to notice Vijay and sense the turmoil within.

David Duncan says: "As ambassadors of the kingdom, we need to be discerning and carry the Father's heart of love that we might bring inner healing to those we encounter."

Rajan was becoming incredibly hardened by the way life had treated him that he had almost become an atheist. He went through such painful and terrible experiences in his past that brought him to a place where he stopped believing in God. He felt no one would pay any attention to his point of view, which did not help the way he had been feeling.

I remember reading in one of John Ortberg's books that: "Dr. James Lynch, co-director of the Psychophysiological Clinic and Laboratories of the University of Maryland, has studied about 'attention'. He discovered that a genuine

Chapter Fourteen

healing of the cardiovascular system takes place when we listen. Studies revealed the blood pressure rises when people speak and lowers when they listen."

John Ortberg himself says: "Attention is the most powerful force in the world. One of the greatest miracles in life is that God pays attention to us. Love pays attention! I believe the work of love is the work of paying attention. Love notices. Love listens. Attention is valuable when we don't give it, we PAY attention. I believe only when we get close enough to catch their pain will they be close enough to catch our love."

Even though these two brothers were feeling God had forgotten them and turned His face from them, it was not true. God in His own way and time reassured Rajan and Vijay that He does indeed care for them! He has counted every tear they have shed. He feels their pain! He has a new day for them; a new dawn; a new blessing. He will do a new thing in their lives.

And it was here at this point in their lives that I was called to be HIS love to them. I was to love them out of whatever was causing such pain, and allow the healing love of Jesus to flow through me, into them.

I shared with dear Rajan that I've experienced a lot of heartache and tears on my path with God as well, and it was hard to believe and confusing to understand at times. However, it has been an amazing journey. His grace saw me through the difficult times. Through these trials, I learnt to trust God in ALL circumstances.

The Lord gave me a heart that was sensitive to Rajan's misery. I became able to sense his pain and could feel that for years he had been inwardly bleeding in silence. God calls us to be sensitive to the pain others are going through. Even without their sharing anything out loud, we are able to simply discern it.

I believe when we become so in tune with God that His heart begins to beat within our chest and we naturally begin to develop the ability to see past a person's disguise and peer deep into their very soul. In my journey through life, I have met so many people with deep scars, both old and fresh. Sometimes just by seeing their face, I am able to observe they are in deep pain inside.

I remember one morning when I had gone to the grocery store. My eyes went to one of the boys who worked there.

I approached him and quietly said, "I know you are going through some deep pain. Don't worry, God will see you through."

Chapter Fourteen

He immediately dropped what he was doing and came over to me, then asked me with great surprise how I could have possibly known he was going through a heartbreaking situation right at that moment, since he had never shared anything with me.

I told him that I felt something was wrong when I saw his face. He replied by saying if God had not sent me that morning to encourage him with what I had said about God seeing him through, that he would have gone into deep depression. I told him that I will be praying for him. This was an encounter that lasted only a few minutes before we went our separate ways again, but a life was changed that day. To God be all the glory, great things HE has done!

I believe my job was to simply bring the love of the Father to Rajan, not to tell him what to do or advise him. He longed for someone to sincerely hear him and understand his feelings right then, without passing judgment or acting superior.

I did as I do with many—just listen, be understanding, sympathetic and compassionate. He needed me to genuinely listen and understand what he was feeling. When I did speak, my words to him were few. The love of God, through me, was what he needed the most.

God's words of encouragement that I was led to speak gave him hope. The love of Jesus ministered to him. God's love always wins. It is genuine, unconditional, and excludes nobody. I believe our gentle and loving ways disarm people where the enemy has a foothold in their lives.

Jan Dravecky made a great point: "Don't fall into the trap of giving pat answers or attempting to explain away your friend's suffering.

Simply accept your friend's honesty and respond in honesty. Honesty opens the floodgates to a hurting heart. Honesty allows tears and silence. It allows questions—with or without answers. Honesty gives a hurting heart a safe place to be loved, to grow and to heal."

Dear Rajan began to experience inner healing after he was finally able to be unburdened of the formidable load he was carrying for so many years without relief, knowing he could trust me.

John Ortberg once wisely stated: "Love is what servanthood is all about! Being a servant is all about putting your love into action. God wants to use us as His hands to wash the feet of the world. That's an awesome job.

Chapter Fourteen

Humbling, hard, even frustrating at times, but awesome. That's because every time you give love away, you end up with more, abundantly more, than you gave away to begin with."

By serving these two brothers, I was able to be part of God's plan for their lives.

John Ortberg also stated: "I love to grab a towel and ask God whose feet He wants me to wash each day. When God shows me a need in someone's life, I ask Him for a fresh, imaginative way to fill it."

These two brothers became my good friends because I took the time to get to know all about them. I became very well acquainted with their pain and heartache. I shed tears with them.

Because of Jesus' love flowing through me, they became so special, so dear to my heart. I could tell them how much they meant to Jesus and how deep His love was for them. They were quick to listen, understand and receive because they had seen that love in action!

I could have preached a good sermon to them or counseled them with all the right words but they had undoubtedly already received that before from other well-meaning people.

They needed someone who would instead just listen, understand their pain without judging them, be one with them, love them, and be there for them.

John Ortberg went on to add: "I believe love is never wasted, even if the one you give it to doesn't change—for it changes you. It makes you look more like Jesus!"

Someone once said that to make a difference in the world, let Jesus make a difference in you. Isn't that true? We should never put ourselves in a place of being a judge, deciding for ourselves who is worthy to receive love and who is not. God loves the world, the whole world, every single individual—even the ones who have chosen not to believe in Him. Isn't that reason enough for us to try and do the same?

I could not answer all the questions Rajan had because he believed God did not exist. His wounds ran deep, but I had the cure—the love of Jesus. That love breaks down every barrier, heals the brokenhearted, makes all things new. I gave him myself and my time, unconditionally. I let him know I cared. I made sure he knew I had no agenda, nor did I want anything from him. Rajan asked me how I could care so much for him. I told him it's Jesus. He was then willing to believe and receive this life-changing love.

Chapter Fourteen

If we accept others without judging them and reach out to them with love, this draws people to us! We can lead them to the One who is LOVE.

Although Rajan has not yet accepted Jesus as his personal Savior, he has accepted His love, and he loves Him as well! He reads the Bible, comes to spend time with me, and also attends the prayer meetings at my place whenever he is able to. God is at work in him and the progress may be slow, but it's sure. God is making a difference in his life!

Kenneth C. Haugk once stated: "Through actions of love, God reaches down and touches people with His power. My caring provides a channel through which God's love can flow. My words and actions of love concretely demonstrate the good news. Through my caring I make the Christian message become something to hear about and something to be seen and touched. Through my actions I give flesh and bones to God's good news."

The Lord has drawn Vijay into a new intimacy with Him and is using him mightily for His glory in his church. He has experienced a breakthrough in his workplace and the favor of God is resting upon him in a special way.

The Lord has brought about a new day in both Vijay and Rajan's lives and I believe He will enable them to experience His love in even greater measure.

Heidi Baker once said: " When you refuse to stop loving, no matter the cost, the gospel is preached beautifully." Our life should become an act meant to display His love. Many people look up to us as a strong example of what being a follower of Jesus is all about. May they see the Father's love through us! Isn't that what Jesus was all about anyway? I pray our lives will reflect the love of Jesus accurately to many. May we continue to magnify the Lord in everything that we do, and everywhere we go, as we boldly proclaim the passionate love of God that we have experienced, and want others to discover.

CHAPTER FIFTEEN

Moved by Compassion

Once a friend and I visited a city which had beautiful beaches. One evening as we were walking around the beach we decided to sit down on a bench for a while and just enjoy the beauty of God's nature that surrounded us. There were a lot of people around.

Suddenly my eyes fell on a man in the midst of the crowd who had painted his whole body—even his eyelids—and was dressed up like Mahatma Gandhi, the leader of the nationalist movement against the British rule of India. He was even holding a walking stick and wore the same eyeglasses, and looked so much like Gandhi that he was the center of attraction for all. As he passed by, everyone would give him a little money.

Soon he was headed our way. As he approached, he stretched out his hand towards us, expecting some money. I looked into his face and could see in his eyes that something had happened that caused him deep pain. The wounded look was unmistakable and my heart went out to him.

I desired to talk with him, get to know him better and know more about his background and why he was doing what he was doing. The Lord helped me to SEE the real man behind the disguise, whom everyone else was ignoring. No one was concerned about what made him paint his body and try so hard to look so convincingly like Gandhi, although they certainly admired how great a job he had done to transform himself.

In today's world, all of us can be so caught up with ourselves that no one has the time to think about another person except if that person has done something for us, as was the case with this young man. He looked amazing! I asked him who he was and why he was begging. He was young and smart and could easily get a job somewhere.

I wanted to know why at his age that he needed to ask for money. He was astonished when I asked him, and when he realized I was genuinely concerned about the REAL HIM, he was moved. We had him sit on the bench with us, and soon tears appeared in his eyes and he began to open up and share about himself.

He was from another city and had been in love with a girl in his hometown. They had planned to get married but the girl's parents were against the idea.

Chapter Fifteen

The girl's brothers threatened his life when they physically attacked him one day. Luckily he was able to get away, and he fled from that city to where we were now. He had no way to sustain himself, so he thought of this idea of transforming into Gandhi, which he knew would attract attention and hopefully bring in some money so he could at least buy something to eat and other necessities.

I was confused and asked him why he had not just gotten a job. He looked educated enough to find something that would pay well and would not have to beg for whatever little money he could get by doing what he was doing now.

He replied sadly that when he ran away from his hometown, to save his life after he was being pursued, that he had had no time to go home and collect his identification records, educational certificate and other documents that he would need to show a potential employer that he would be worthy of a good job. He had changed his name, his hairstyle and how he looked when he had fled, because he was worried that if someone recognized him that they would inform the brothers of the girl that he loved about his whereabouts, and they would attempt to find him here and kill him again.

STOP FOR THE ONE

My eyes filled with tears as I heard this precious homeless man's sad story. He knew my friend and I were genuinely concerned, so he trusted us and shared his real name and who his family is. He then asked me if I was a priest of some church. I was taken aback by that question and asked him why he said that.

He replied that he had heard that priests are very warm and caring, and he could sense the love of Jesus within us as we talked. He had also noticed how we gave him all of our attention, and took the time to make him sit with us and patiently listen. He himself had been touched by the tears in my eyes as he shared his story.

I told him that I am a lover of Jesus and a servant of God and I've given my life to Jesus to just "love on people." He took my hand and bowed his head, letting my hand touch his forehead. He sat and listened to me as I shared with him how much Jesus loves him. I told him that Jesus had a special plan for his life and future, and He arranged a divine meeting so we could tell him about it. I assured him that God loves him, prayed protection over his life and told him that Jesus has a wonderful future for him.

I told him to cast all his cares on Jesus and trust Him with his life and for his protection and future. He was listening very attentively.

Chapter Fifteen

Finally he spoke. "I know now that God brought both of you here to me because He truly loves me! This is the first time ever that someone SAW the real me behind my disguise and stopped me to inquire how I am, then listened to my hurting heart. Everyone is so busy that no one has time for anyone else in this world. But here you are, giving me all your time and attention as if I am important." He stopped for a moment, then continued: "I had begun to feel that life had no meaning. I was so down and out that there seemed to be no reason to live. Not only have you encouraged and comforted me, but you have given me hope and the strength to not give up."

I love the words by Haddon Robinson: "Making a conscious effort to hear—it is essential to a helping relationship. If I were asked to choose the single most important skill for counselors, it would be the ability to listen. The only reason some people have a secret sorrow is that the rest of us won't take time to listen to them."

Praise God that He took us to that city at the right time, to the exact place, to reach out to this precious homeless, lonely man with His love, encouragement, and hope!

God had this dear person on His heart and He found my friend and I available to use to BE His LOVE to him.

John Ortberg said: "The main place you do the work of God is as you walk along. It doesn't have to be in high profile, important positions. It will happen, if it happens at all, in the routine, unspectacular corners of your life. As you walk along."

I know I am repeating myself, but I will say it again. When a person is going through agony deep within their soul, all he wants is somebody to just be there for him. To sit with him, listen to him, and put an arm around his shoulder and cry with him.

Jill and Judy Briscoe put it this way: "LOVE NOURISHES. Love smiles at strangers. Love walks hot streets finding cold drinks for tired throats. Love that is love has muscles, they are grown-doing love. Love never counts the miles walked so it never notices the extra one, love laughs and cries. Love persists like a disciplined athlete determined to win the crown for costly caring."

I feel so deeply for the broken ones that God brings our way! We ignore them, or do not spend quality time with them. How true are the words of a precious dear woman of God, Mary Lindow: "Do you just kick it out of the way and go on? Often we see someone much like the little dead sparrow, wounded or suffering from the cruelty of others too busy to really care about a "broken wing" or perhaps a broken heart."

Chapter Fifteen

There are so many people in this world with deep hidden wounds and they desperately are searching for someone with whom they can share their pain, and lessen the hurt inside.

Sadly, there are very few people who are sensitive to the tears and hidden cries of these hearts that are all around them. Even if we do realize the person in front of us is afflicted and desolate, do we take whatever time is needed to listen and bring about real change in that life?

These encounters with people may well be direct interventions from God Himself, meant to start these people on a road to recovering their health!

I thank God for the inverted blessing of the initial years of my walk with Him, when I was struggling, rejected, and wounded. There was no shortage of people who came my way who were willing to give me a good sermon, excellent advice, or wonderful counseling, but no one really took time to just listen to my deepest hurts and wounds.

No one lent a sympathetic ear and let me just talk about that which was bothering me the most and causing deep inner turmoil. I was left to fight my own battles with no one by my side to encourage and lift me—BUT GOD!

Yes, I badly needed someone to really understand me and love me in spite of my shortcomings, but all I received was well meaning counseling, sermons and advice. How I longed for a safe place to be myself, to cry if need be, without fear of chastisement—just someone to CARE, that I knew would simply be there when I needed him the most. I never received this!

Because I was left to fend for myself, I am now able to give what I was never given. To those who are wounded I give my all: my time, my undivided attention, the care and love I wished I had had!

I allow people to feel at home with me, and I encourage them to freely share what is on their heart without admonishment or judgment. I want them to know I will journey with them in their anguish so they know they are never alone. In other words, I am simply loving them with the love of Jesus—loving them as He loves me.

The undeniable and reliable power of Jesus' love can then flow into their inner being like a healing balm that soothes the pain and enables them to begin to become whole once again.

Our new friend, whose name incidentally was Ramesh, had sat with us and not only poured out his heart but was attentive to all we spoke to him.

Chapter Fifteen

He did not impatiently wait for us to finish then rush to get up and go collect more money from the crowd. Instead, he was so enraptured in our fellowship and time together that he experienced God's love, peace and healing in a very practical and life-altering way. For once he felt he was important, understood, loved and cared for.

After much time together, I prayed for him and as I was speaking, he bowed his head with humility and reverence. After prayer, he took my hand once more and touched his forehead.

The Lord had touched his heart through my obedience and desire to be HIS hands, HIS feet, HIS heart. I quietly put some money into his shirt pocket, and when he took it out and saw what it was, he was so thrilled. He said he no longer needed to go and beg for money. He thanked us, then went away happily and full of joy. We assured him of our prayers.

I was so overjoyed that I could show God's love to dear Ramesh in a down-to-earth way and also share with him my testimony and give him the Good News that Jesus loves him with an everlasting love. I believe the Lord met with him and eternity will show what God did through that divine meeting with dear Ramesh, one day near the sea shore.

STOP FOR THE ONE

God wants us to SHOW His love to everyone He brings our way or takes us to. He wishes for us to also provide for all those who are lying alongside the road in a state of hopelessness, despair and great need. You may never fully realize how much you have to offer until you see how deep the needs of these people are.

I also believe it is not only just praying for a person but practically meeting them at the exact point of their need that is so important as well. Ramesh undoubtedly did need love and encouragement, but he also was in great need of finances due to what had happened to him. We should always be sensitive and pray for discernment to help the person with what their actual palpable need might be. It could be physical hunger, so take the person to a restaurant and feed him. It could be financial, so give them some money to help them on their way.

Another memory comes to mind. I remember one time as I was driving my motorbike that I saw a person lying by the roadside. He was having an epileptic seizure.

A few people had gathered around him and were trying to help. One of them gave him a piece of iron to hold and after he grabbed it, the seizures stopped and he was able to sit and talk normally. Everyone left shortly after this, but I stayed with him.

Chapter Fifteen

I asked about his problem. He said he was on medication for the epilepsy. He had just come from the hospital, and showed me the doctor's prescription then sadly told me that he had no money to buy the medicines. He said these medicines are available only in the bigger and well known pharmacies which the closest one was far distant. I told him to sit with me on my motorbike and together we went to the medical shop and bought him what he needed. I could have given him the money for his medication then felt I had helped him enough and left, but I always do as the Spirit of God leads, not what I sometimes feel like doing, myself.

It is important to constructively help a person where they need help the most and not solely give the gospel to the poor and needy, then send them on their way without any tenable aid.

I am not saying you must help everyone who crosses your path in this way, but you do need to be sensitive and discerning in how to help, and when. There are times we meet dishonest people who would take advantage of us without thinking twice. We need to be wise and not give in to such people, but pray and exercise discernment, then take steps to help if the Lord is leading us to. God desires for us to have a character full of love and mercy.

J. Daniel Lupton writes: "Jesus was anointed and commissioned by God's Spirit for a special ministry to the poor [see Luke 4:18-19]. He was called to care for the needy, and He expects us to share that calling. He instructed us, 'But when you give a banquet, invite the poor... and you will be blessed... although they cannot repay you.' [Luke 14:13-14].

"The first church at Jerusalem asked Paul to remember the poor which was the very thing he was eager to do. [Galatians 2:10]. Jesus specialized in helping and healing the wounded. The people brought to Jesus all had various kinds of sicknesses, and laying His hands on each one, He healed them. [Luke 4:40].

"He passionately preached good news to those who were overwhelmed by all the bad news. He brought liberation to people who were bound by sin and demons. Jesus made Himself available, healing hands and eyes, feeding the hungry, defending the accused, and associating with the disreputable. Humanity marked everything Jesus accomplished for the poor and needy; He remembered that His human roots began with the poor in a stable."

Reaching the hurting, sharing Jesus with those who need Him, and serving Him with all I am and all I have is the goal of my life and ministry.

Chapter Fifteen

I would like to close with these words by Michele Perry: "Love has eyes to see royalty along the roadside and glory hidden in the unexpected gutters of life. Jesus desires the destinies of those who have been trampled and tossed aside to be restored to their full beauty. His love washes us clean, and His grace makes us new. He calls each of us in from the roadsides of life to come home to His heart. And until we find our place in His heart, we will never truly be at home."

STOP FOR THE ONE

CHAPTER SIXTEEN

From the Depths of Despair to Heights of Joy

Great power resides within the Holy Word of God and the testimony of our brethren.

Through sharing our experiences, we not only bring glory to God but deliver hope to each other as we travel down life's road together.

You have read some incredible testimonies of lives changed forever after experiencing the love of Jesus, through me, His humble servant.

Now I will share my personal story in hopes of allowing you to understand exactly how I am able to feel others' pain so deeply and display my Lord's love so passionately.

STOP FOR THE ONE

I have heard it said that: "There's no other story like yours! Only you can share it. If you don't, it'll be lost forever. You may not be a Bible scholar, you are the authority of your life. Actually, your testimony is more effective than a sermon. People lose interest when you quote theologians, but they have a natural curiosity about experiences they've never had. So, all you must do is use your story to build a bridge that Jesus can walk across into their heart."

In my first book, "Lost and Found," I shared my testimony about how I came to know the Lord Jesus Christ as my personal Saviour and Lord, after being raised in a devout Hindu household. I also mentioned how I was delivered from the serious physical ailments I have always struggled with all my life. Now, I will dive deeper into what happened to me in the days, months, and years following my decision to follow Jesus.

In the beginning, everyone at home was very happy that Jesus had delivered me from all the physical problems that I was plagued with, and they noticed how intensely I was enjoying His peace.

They allowed me to go to a Christian church and were even more surprised that I no longer craved the occasional alcoholic drink.

Chapter Sixteen

They definitely noticed this brand-new Ravi, who was at rest and was no longer struggling as before and were content to allow me to live my life as I chose.

However, this would all change when one day it was decided the family would have a Puja, which is a devoted act of worship to a god in whom they believed.

Within my home, it was acceptable to follow Jesus as one of the gods, so long as the follower also believed and followed the gods of the rest of the household. The problem began when I made it clear that I wished to follow Jesus exclusively!

I shared with them that I have found new meaning and purpose in life through Jesus, and His teachings do not allow me to be part of any other faith. I gracefully made sure they fully understood that I was not attempting to compel them to believe what I believe, only asking them to respect my decision as I respected their freedom to worship who and how they chose.

Unfortunately, my words were met with extreme hostility. I was physically beaten by my brother and thrown out of the family home. They said they would have nothing to do with me if I left their religion and followed Christianity.

I tried to explain to them that I had not accepted Christianity the religion, but Christ the Person, and there was a great difference between them. Nevertheless, I found myself out on my own—with bare feet and only the shirt on my back and the promises of my Lord to sustain me.

I had no idea where to go or what to do. The Lord led me to go to Bangalore where my sister, Sangeeta, and her family lived. I took a job in Bangalore and stayed with Sangeeta. She knew of my decision to follow Jesus, and the peace it brought me. She was a very staunch Hindu as the rest of my family was, and like them she too did not agree with my decision.

However, she was kind to me because she was upset by the way my brothers had treated me. I found a church nearby and enjoyed going there.

After coming home from work in the evening, I would go to the Bible study and prayer meetings the church held during the week. Sangeeta noticed I was spending much time studying the Bible, and was getting more involved with church.

One night as we were all at the dinner table having our meal together, she asked me if I had been baptized and I replied that I had.

Chapter Sixteen

She was furious and immediately asked me to get out of her house so I would not influence her children. My kind brother-in-law asked her to leave me alone to live my life as I chose, but she would not back down. I, along with only my bag of meager possessions, left her home. Again, I was faced with having nowhere to go.

I chose to believe that the God who had tenderly wooed me to Him, would again provide what I needed. I called and spoke to a dear pastor friend of mine, the Reverend Vinay Moses and told him what I had gone through. He was so kind and gracious, and asked me to come and stay with him. I was touched but told him that I wished to be alone as I desired to spend more time in God's presence.

He arranged for me to stay in a Christian retreat centre which was very quiet and had a lovely, peaceful surrounding. I was happy to be there all by myself, alone with my Lord. It was not easy, BUT GOD!

Sangeeta, in the meantime, had called the rest of our family and even some of our other relatives and told them about my baptism and how she hated me and would have nothing to do with me. For about a year she did not speak to me and asked me not to visit her or have anything to do with her and her family.

Her children were banned from having any contact with me. Yet through it all, my God stood with me.

About two weeks after I moved into the retreat centre, I attended church one Sunday morning and Pastor Mike Peppin was sharing about Jeremiah 1:5, *"Before I formed you in the womb I knew you, before you were born I set you apart; I appointed you as a prophet to the nations."*

How the Lord spoke through this verse to a heart that needed to hear this message, right then! Immediately I prayed, "Here I am—I give myself to You." And I surrendered my life to serve Him fully. I thank God for His grace that not only enabled me to hear His clear voice, but also helped me to obey Him without hesitation. I had such great joy that I was chosen to serve Him.

The next day as I went to work, I spoke to my boss and told him that I wanted to leave my job because I desired to serve the Lord Jesus full time. He was taken aback, thinking I had gone crazy, but he told me I could go. After I left my job, I was filled with inexpressible joy in my heart to serve the Lord. Not once did I have any thought about how I would serve Him or where the finances would come from. I never panicked and wondered what have I just done—NOT ONCE.

Chapter Sixteen

I had deep peace about my decision to leave all to follow Jesus! I have learnt one thing in my life and that is to simply obey Him and His Word and leave the rest to Him because that is His department and His responsibility. I knew that He is faithful to lead me and provide for me.

The moment Sangeeta heard about me leaving my job to serve God full time, she could not bear it. She called my brothers and asked them to come and take me back to Kolkata. She told them I had gone mad as the Christians had brainwashed me, and I had left my job to serve my God. If they did not come and get me, they would lose me. She also told them that she will not allow me to live in the same city that she lives in, so they must come and get me out of Bangalore.

After staying in the guest house for a month, I started looking for a more permanent place to stay and the Lord was gracious to provide me with one small room. Even though the room was in an area that was very noisy and crowded, I was thankful for it.

Whatever His will was for me—small room or big mansion, clean and quiet area or busy and crowded, I was content. Being in the centre of His will is what I always want.

Soon after I moved into my home, my brother Raj appeared at my doorway. My oldest brother Lalit had heard about my baptism and had angrily called Raj to go to Bangalore to get me. Raj did not give me a chance to speak but ordered me to pack up my things, for he had come to take me back to Kolkata.

When I replied, "I have decided to follow Jesus, no turning back!"

He laughed and replied, "And where have you ended up? This small room that you are staying in—even our servants would not stay in such a room. What has your God done to you? From the family estate where you lived in comfort, He has brought you to this noisy, crowded area and one tiny room. Come back home with me and we will give you whatever you want—money, a home, the luxuries you have always known… only you must give up and leave this faith!"

Raj continued to look around my small room with disdain as he went on belittling my decision and current situation.

I told him that while he was just seeing the crowded, noisy area and tiny room, he couldn't see how God was keeping me in Heavenly places. Yes, the Lord placed me in that small room to humble me!

Chapter Sixteen

I had learned as a young child being raised in a wealthy family that I could summon people who would instantly cater to my demands, and at my command I could receive the pampering one is given, especially as the baby of the family.

Now, being in this small room was teaching me to rely on God and to become strong in Him. I discovered that my life was evolving and that my survival was no longer based on earthly provisions but on spiritual ones. I was enlightened to see that I could survive in a world that was previously thought of as unsurvivable, and desired to share this revelation with others. There was hope and I wanted everyone to know it. I was beginning to know what it was to be hungry, a spiritual hunger that could not be satisfied by man's hands. I wanted to feed the world from God's banquet table.

Raj asked me sarcastically how I would live, and where the money it took to live would come from? After a while, I replied that Jesus has chosen me to serve Him, and He is faithful to care and provide for all my needs. He mocked me again and added that I would now live like a beggar since I was nothing without them. He told me that my identity comes from the Kapoor family. I replied that my identity comes from Jesus. I am a child of the Most High God and He is my Abba Father.

He laughed and said he was sure I had gone mad, since the Christians have brainwashed me. He went on to say that if I did not go back with him, I did not exist anymore for them. My name would not be spoken in their house. If I did not return with him, my inheritance and share of property would not be given to me and even my name would be erased from the family tree. He demanded I sign a paper saying that nothing of my share and property is mine anymore. I told him that I don't need to sign anything, since I give whatever is mine as a gift to them.

Raj was furious and phoned Lalit, telling him he could get nowhere with me, since I had gone completely mad and was a lost cause. Lalit was very loud and yelled at me over the phone, thinking I would get scared as I used to when I was younger, and bow to his demands. I had always been terribly afraid of him. He used to rule, control, and dominate me through force, and I used to shake in fear in front of him. But now? I had the Lord and He was giving me wisdom and boldness to speak. He had released me from every fear and also given me the spirit of power, love and sound mind. That bothered both my brothers as they wondered how I had suddenly become so bold and strong where before I had cowered before them and done all they demanded.

Chapter Sixteen

Raj laughed and said that I would end up on the streets and one day would come crawling on my knees, begging them to take me back. I told him that day will never come but one day God will bring him and all of my family to me for prayer. Raj said if I did not stop this foolishness right then that I would not be allowed to enter Kolkata or even see my mother. I just kept quiet.

It was not easy to go through such an experience, yet I knew then as I know now that Jesus is more precious than anything the world can offer, more valuable than diamonds, lands, property, name, or fame. NOTHING that man desires can ever compare to Him!

After Raj returned to Kolkata without me, both my brothers' actions began to take a toll on my mother, and she became very sick. Upon hearing of her illness, I immediately went to Kolkata to see her. I stayed at my sister Renu's place.

I would visit my mother every morning for an hour or two then come back to Renu's house. All that my brothers were doing to me had a great impact on my dear mother, and one evening her condition became very serious. The doctors came quickly and gave her something to help her sleep. I had no choice but to spend the night there because she needed me.

STOP FOR THE ONE

I was quietly reading a book when my sister-in-law came in and asked me to have dinner with the rest of the family. I replied that I'd already eaten at Renu's home. She quietly asked me to please reconsider and just eat a little something, otherwise Lalit will create a big scene. I told her again that I had already eaten.

Sure enough, after a while Lalit stormed into the room and demanded I have dinner. When I repeated what I had told my sister-in-law, he started shouting. I asked him to keep his voice down since our mother was not doing well and should not be disturbed. He replied in the same loud voice that he did not care even if she dies, for if that happened, it will be because of me.

Perhaps I should mention that before I had come to the Lord and while I was still living at home in Kolkata, Lalit often came home from the office in the evening and would start drinking. He became loud and demanding and most times would begin to go on and on about me.

My mother would tell me to leave the house after he came back from work because he would go off on me without any reason, and she worried about me. I began to leave home every night around 8 PM, go to Renu's place and have dinner there, then come back home around midnight when Lalit was sleeping.

Chapter Sixteen

After I accepted Jesus, his ranting became even worse. I tried very much to avoid any kind of confrontation or give him any reason to become even angrier.

I heard my mother calling for me, and I rushed into her room and locked it from inside. She was upset, wondering what was going on. I explained to her that my brothers wanted to insult, ridicule, and humiliate me.

I told her to be strong and reassured her that all was well, then prayed over her. The Lord strengthened her, and she told me to leave for Renu's house the next morning, and not to come back here to stay again since she would be fine. I was relieved that my mother had been strengthened by the Lord, and I decided it would be safe to leave her alone to sleep.

I went into the dining room and saw everyone was together, and drinking. My sister-in-law immediately placed a plate of food in front of me. After I quietly thanked her but again refused, Lalit got up from his chair, obviously heavily intoxicated and using a very loud voice. He threw the plate of food, then flipped the dining room table upside down. He was very angry. There was a big picture of The Last Supper hanging on the wall which Renu had given Lalit some time ago.

Immediately, he went over to the picture, tore it off the wall and was about to break it, saying he would not allow this "God" to be in the home. I just silently watched him and said nothing. I went back to my mother's room, and this time Lalit followed. He broke the glass of the dressing table, then hit me and tore my clothes before going back to the others. He began drinking again and saying all kinds of things against me and kept on going until around midnight.

It was sad that neither Raj, his wife, my sisters, or brothers-in-law would stand up to Lalit when he was on a rampage, because they were all afraid of him. No one spoke up for me, so I had to bear the insults and beatings alone.

The next morning, I once again prayed for my mother and told her to be strong and I left to be with Renu at her house. I decided to visit my mother during the day while Lalit was at work. I would go home and see her for about an hour, then head back to Renu's home.

My brothers wanted to make more trouble with me, so they started calling Renu, demanding I come to the house. I told her to tell them I refuse to see them. My brothers could not bear that I had not given into their demands.

Chapter Sixteen

They thought they could bribe me with money so they told Renu to ask me what I wanted, so they could give me some money then send me away. Renu replied that I did not want anything from them, then added that I had forgiven them for all they had done to me.

After about four or five days of me visiting my Mother while they were at work, my mother said she was doing much better and asked me not to visit anymore since she was worried Lalit's anger would flare up again.

After seeing my mother strengthened and recovering, I left Kolkata with a heavy heart full of deep anguish. Yet because of Jesus' abiding presence and His perfect peace that passes all understanding, I was at rest.

Life on my own, living out of my small room with no steady income, was not easy. I did go through VERY difficult times. I lived off rice and pickles for days. On other days, there was nothing to eat. God allowed all of this to see if I really meant business when I said I love Him and would serve Him, come what may.

The Lord taught me to never mention my needs to anyone, but only to Him in prayer, trusting Him for the provisions I needed. I took my eyes off people and fixed my gaze solely on Him. He taught me to live on faith.

Truthfully, I had expected persecution and insults from my brothers because I had embraced Jesus. I knew them and the Hindu religion well enough to know they would not willingly accept my decision. What totally surprised me, however, was the lack of support from fellow Christians who would encourage and strengthen me.

I had nobody that I could freely share my hurting heart with! When I shared with one or two believers about all I had gone through with my family, the only thing I received was sermons and preaching. No one really listened. No one wanted to take the time to understand. Nobody encouraged me for taking a stand for my faith as I had.

The same people who sat with me in church and heard the same sermons or sang the same songs about living for Jesus and having faith were asking me how I expected to live without a job—even just part time, to bring some money in, then serve the Lord with whatever time and money I had left over. They started counseling me or telling me to pray and get confirmation from the Lord about my calling.

The same people who prayed along with me about the harvest being plentiful and labourers few now felt the need to tell me to get back to work.

Chapter Sixteen

They were unable to accept the idea of someone who fully trusted the Lord to provide. There were times when people at church would not introduce me to others because when asked what I was doing, they would be embarrassed to say that I simply have a call to serve the Lord.

I was faithfully attending church, both the Sunday service and the meetings throughout the week. After being put down by those I talked to time after time, I began to stop going to church. My family had rejected me and treated me badly for my faith, and now the experience I had had with members of God's family was heartbreaking. Was there anyone out there who would BE the Jesus we were all hearing about in church and reading about in the Bible? If ever I needed a shoulder to cry on, a hand to hold, or even just someone to listen, it was then.

Emotionally, physically, and mentally I'd gone through a lot. To move away from all relationships with other people, to be secluded and living all by yourself, and to serve Him without any one to stand by you is not easy. Going through the valley of shadow of death without having anyone to comfort and encourage you is not easy. To have many questions but no one there to answer them is not easy.

STOP FOR THE ONE

I used to dread the knock at my door, wondering who's come now to try to make me come to my senses. There were people who would come and stay for hours. Not to listen, but to speak from the Word of God against my situation. I would wonder how they were not more sensitive or discerning. Did they not pray to the Lord for wisdom before coming?

Some of them went on and on for hours, giving me the message they felt I needed to hear. There was not even ONE who came to encourage me and say they were so thankful that God had chosen me to go out into the harvest field.

Nobody stood with me in prayer. Nobody sympathized with all I had gone through with my family, after having left all to follow Jesus. Didn't anyone have enough of the love of Christ within their own heart to sense a brother's agony and comfort him?

In His presence and His presence alone, I learnt what it was to depend completely on Him. All the rejection and hurt I received compelled me to turn away from all human help and seek the help of Jesus alone.

And then, one day, the Lord divinely connected me with a Christian brother, Norton, who became a great encouragement to me.

Chapter Sixteen

He loved the Lord with all his heart and was serious about his walk with God. He was a dedicated lover of books and he used to take me to the book shops and Christian book exhibitions.

I began to take notice of which authors' books he was picking up. He was a great inspiration to me. He was a great example of the love of Jesus and I could definitely see Christ working in his life. We shared so many great times of fellowship but sadly, they were cut short. Within two years, he went to be with the Lord. After he went to glory, I was once again left alone. I took my concerns to the Lord. "Lord, You sent this precious brother to me, and I had just begun to collect myself.

There was so much to learn from Him and now with his sudden passing, I feel great despair in my life. His family was very close to me. I used to visit them often we would pray for and encourage each other.

Brother Norton had introduced me to great authors like A.W. Tozer, Spurgeon, D.L Moody, Charles Finney, Wesley, Andrew Murray, William Booth, David Brainard and so many others who shared amazing testimonies as men and women of God. I was reading wonderful books by authors whose subject matter was so deep that I felt my own faith stretch and grow as I turned each page.

The Lord ministered to me through each one of them. For a new believer, to understand Watchman Nee, Jesse Penn Lewis, or Madame Guyon, was nothing but by the sheer grace of God.

For you see—I had only studied up to the 8th grade/standard in school! Imagine how someone like this could ever understand all the deep themes in advanced books such as these. I had been a brilliant student but due to my ongoing physical problems in my younger days, I had to discontinue my studies.

Here in my solitude, the Lord encouraged me to be a book lover, and He amazed me many times by bringing the right book at the right time that provided the exact answers to many of my questions, and helped me in my journey. I used to shut myself in my room with Him and spend many days in His presence in fasting and prayer. I just LOVED to be with Him. I would spend a lot of time in worship and prayer and reading the Bible.

During that season of my life, the Lord brought brother Ravi Zacharias to mind so I began to get audio tapes of his messages and his books. I could not get enough! I fully immersed myself in his messages. I remember with deep joy how our Lord directed and enabled me to attend a meeting of brother Ravi in Kolkata. Brother Ravi shared his personal testimony about his life.

Chapter Sixteen

I felt right then that the Lord was confirming everything would be all right in my life, as I heard what He had done in the life of brother Ravi. Since then, there has been NO turning back for me.

I remember praying, "Lord, D.L. Moody once said, 'The world has yet to see what God can do with one man, fully yielded to Him.' I want to be that man, fully yielded to You. Here I am, with all I am, I surrender all to You. I want to always depend upon You, learn from You, and Your Word. Please teach me, counsel me, correct me, discipline me, and bring me to a place of complete submission to Your will and purposes."

Oh, there's SO MUCH that I went through on my journey. My message to you is not to highlight the pain but to let you know what I learnt through persecution and suffering. The Lord turned things around for good! *"And we know that in all things God works for the good of those who love him, who have been called according to his purpose."* (Romans 8:28)

Every bad thing that happened to me taught me valuable lessons and brought me closer to His heart. I am devoted to and desire Him and only Him. I am burdened for souls. I am submitted and yielded to Him alone, desiring only His Name to be glorified in and through my life.

We have received the gift of God's forgiveness. Jesus died and gave each one of us a gift of forgiveness; we simply need to receive it. In the same way we need to forgive those who've hurt us, we need to give them a gift of forgiveness.

This is the first step towards freedom from emotional pain. Those who I have forgiven definitely didn't deserve it, but I had a choice: I could either be imprisoned by pain or forgive and trust that God would work things out. He's worked things out in so many ways, it still amazes me.

My brothers threw me out. I used what they did in forgiving them and praying for them. When I would go to my hometown and they would not want to see me, I would visit them anyway, smile at them and hold nothing against them in my heart.

The love that the Lord enabled me to show my brothers convicted them. They were amazed to see how the grace of Jesus had changed me and how I held no bad feelings towards them for their actions.

Instead, they saw me living out my faith and inwardly leaning on God and God alone, regardless of what happened to me outwardly. Jesus extended mercy to those who ridiculed Him and spat on Him.

Chapter Sixteen

In the midst of being tortured and ultimately hung on a cross to die, He still loved them. It is said that it was His LOVE that held Him on the cross. How could I, His humble servant, not also love and extend mercy to those who treated me shamefully? I am not greater than my Master and Savior. I want my life to model His life in every way.

Someone asked Francis of Assisi how he was able to accomplish so much. He replied, "This may be why: The Lord looked down from heaven and said, 'Where can I find the weakest, littlest man on earth? Then He saw me and said, 'I've found him. I will work through him, and he won't be proud of it. He'll see that I am only using him because of his insignificance."(Taken from the devotional "Our Daily Bread")

The Lord called me to serve Him full time. Yes, by His grace, I instantly obeyed but I did think, "Why me, Lord? I am hardly educated and am a simple, ordinary person with no special talents or skills."

The Lord said, "I have chosen you to show the world what I can do through a lowly, common person who loves Me." How true that His expectation is not from what we can do for Him, but from Himself—what He can do in, with, and through us!

For many years, my family did not have any communication with me. Sangeeta would not allow her children to speak with me and would often ask me to leave. I respected her wishes and would go, but a few days later I would visit again. I continued to pray for all of them and show them the Lord's kindness and love.

The day finally came when my brothers asked me to forgive them for all they had done to me!

They now call me and ask for prayer. Many relatives, including those who mistreated me so cruelly in the past, also call and ask me to pray for them. The Lord also touched Sangeeta and brought about a radical change in her life.

Today she also calls me and asks for prayer. She is a very gifted artist and has made several beautiful paintings, including one of the Cross, which now hang in my house!

They mean so much to me. My love alone could never have made such a change in her life. The only love that reached Sangeeta liberally and unreservedly was the love of Christ. I know, because I was also smitten by that unconditional love, and a deep desire for others to know it, as well. It is a life changer!

Chapter Sixteen

I have learnt what Paul meant when he said in Philippians 4:11-12: *"I have learned to be content whatever the circumstances. I know what it is to be in need, and I know what it is to have plenty. I have learned the secret of being content in any and every situation, whether well fed or hungry, whether living in plenty or in want."*

Due to my own trials, I am able to live anywhere, eat anything, and survive in any condition. I have learnt to do with or without food, for there have been plenty of times I had no choice. I feel for the needy ones who do not have food to eat. I'm burdened for them. I love to reach out to them, for I know how they feel. God took me through many years of training and preparation. This "preparation period" can be the most difficult time of your life, for the process burns away all that cannot be used by Him.

Yet through it all it also teaches we must TRUST Him to use every experience for our good! Pastor Jim Cymbala once said, "God uses the bruises and heartbreaks in our lives so we can have compassion on others, so we can feel what God feels for them."

After the four long years of living in my small room, the Lord blessed me with a bigger home, and enabled me to have a prayer group there. For many years now we have met every Saturday. We fast and pray and intercede on behalf of others. I have seen and continue to see the power of God through answered prayers.

Intercession has become my lifestyle. I just love to be on my knees, advocating for those I am led to pray for!

I thank God now for when those I counted as friends deserted me, leaving me all alone. Yes, I lost many people that I once cared for, but in the process, I have grown.

My heart in this matter can perhaps best be expressed by these words I once read: "I used to be afraid of losing people until I realized most of them were never really there for me anyway. Even though my loyalty and love for them ran deep, they couldn't care less. So instead of being afraid of losing them, I fell back and watched them lose me. This is growth."

I couldn't find a hand to hold or a shoulder to cry on when I needed it, but I thank God for He birthed a ministry where I give to others what I didn't get myself.

I don't preach to people in pain, loneliness, or depression. I give them myself—my hand to hold and my shoulder to cry on. I do not ask a wounded person how he feels, for I already know. I feel with them.

Chapter Sixteen

I am anguished by their pain. I am able to weep with them because I profoundly empathize!

I have had a lot of attacks on my ministry. Instead of seeing these as a personal offense, I use them to yield myself more and more in prayer. I have learnt to let nothing get me down, except down on my knees. I have learnt a lot from my mistakes and failures.

One thing in particular that I have learnt from the Lord is to be open to correction. I once heard that "those things, and those people, that are well-tested are of the greatest use!"

God has brought so many amazing men and women of God into my life that challenge and convict me to become an even better servant of His. He brought books by amazing authors that have blessed my life.

The enemy thought my education was over, all those many years ago when I was forced to drop out of school due to my physical problems, but little did he know that one day the Lord would enable me to write for Him. And the Lord has been gracious in enabling me to bring out my first book, 'Lost and Found" in 2019, and now this one that you are reading.

I give glory to the Lord for it is not about how much we have studied and how much we know; or the title, money and position we hold—but it's all about Him, in Whom we have believed. I desire for the Lord to use me to reach many people through the story of my life and testimony, and my pen in many parts of the world where I cannot physically go and share.

Satan thought he could steal and destroy my future, but he did not know that the Lord would use me in not only reaching out to people in India, but far and beyond to every nation through my writing for Him.

I want people to see and believe Jesus through the living testimonies in my life and the lives of the great saints in the Bible that walked in complete dependence on HIM.

The testimonies of those lives inspired me. I told the Lord that He did it for them, and since He is the same yesterday, today, and forever, that I believe He will do it for me too. And, sure enough, He did!

I could fill an entire book with just stories of how God reached out to me at my lowest and most desperate times of need, and how much He has been good and faithful to me. I laid it all on the line and fully immersed myself in His promises to never leave me and to always be all I needed, as I launched into serving Him full time.

Chapter Sixteen

Yes, in the back of my mind the words of my family still played, that I would be homeless and living on the streets, then come crawling back on my knees, begging to them. The doubts of the Christian people who asked where my finances would come from or how I would sustain myself also came to mind from time to time, but I knew my God was bigger than these problems.

God does not call a person into service for Him, then turn His back on him. Yes, it has been hard. There have been a lot of heartaches and tears on this path with God, which can be hard and confusing at times.

But, it has been an amazing journey. Someone once said, "We don't make it through tough times. We are made through tough times—made into the beauty of Christ Jesus." There is so much that I have indeed lost, yet in His sight gained much more, and so will you! I was brought closer to God and became stronger and wiser through all the experiences He allowed in my life. I learned submission and yielding to His will and not mine; to surrender my motives and heart's desires.

The Holy Spirit did a meticulous open-heart surgery and brought inner healing to every part that was wounded and broken. He formed us with His tender hands, and He specializes in healing us.

It did not happen overnight, no, but what He begins, He always completes. Our God takes the broken pieces, the utterly shattered remnants of our former lives, and redeems and creates something new and beautiful within us.

Joseph M. Stowell said, "God never wastes our sorrows. In Him, there is certain purpose in pain. There are the purposes of conformity to His image, usability in His service, purity in our lives, a new sense of God-sufficiency, effectiveness in ministry, and identity with Christ."

Because I refused to allow others' words to cause me to become bitter and unforgiving, God has allowed me to be used to counsel some of those who once felt I would never be of use to anyone.

Others have heard about how I trusted God and determined to minister to others full-time with no turning back, and I am seeing the fruit of this extreme step of faith as lives are being reached and changed for Him.

One pastor, who was struggling with a personal matter in his family, used to call me and share his heart. He was a pastor with a very large congregation and would always tell me that while he was the pastor of such a sizable church that I was his pastor. God was using me to be a pastor to the pastors! I was humbled by his words.

A family who had been encouraged by the Lord through my ministry would arrange a meeting and ask me to lead it. They told me once that they had a church pastor, but I was their family pastor. They knew I was only a phone call away whenever they needed prayer or just someone to be there.

Another time I got a call from a man who shared his heart-breaking story and wanted advice and prayer. I prayed for him, then spoke what the Spirit of God led me to say. Later, when I asked him what he does for a living, he said he is a professional counselor.

Do not get me wrong. I am not trying to boast about myself or look to men for approval. My point is that even though my family, fellow believers and men and women of God all gave up on me, GOD had better plans for my life. When we surrender our will to His and give Him free reign to mould, shape, and forge us into the vessel He wants us to be: the beautiful finished work our Lord produces from the unalluring lump of clay we once were can be used in ways nobody ever thought possible.

It amazes, surprises, and at times even humiliates those who were once so outspoken about our worthlessness.

I agree with the words of Michele Perry from her book, "Love has a Face," "Every rejection in my life has actually been a protection by His love. Every setback is a setup for something greater. Everything meant to harm and destroy turned into that which has strengthened and built me into who I now am."

Over the years I have come to know my sweet Lord Jesus in deeper levels than I have ever known Him before. The toils of my life, the struggles of my past, and the mockery and ridicule I faced all faded away when I realized that God in His Divine plan was drawing me closer to His heart. It is only through crushing that the fragrance emerges. Mary broke her alabaster box of precious ointment and the fragrance pleased the Lord. It was not just the breaking, it was also the making of a new heart. In my case, it birthed an empathetic ministry that has made me very sensitive to how people feel. He gives me the grace to walk gently with those in extreme pain, and help them experience the healing, all-encompassing love of Jesus.

I love the words of Bob Sorge, "God raises you up, the impact of your story will derive more from your cross season than your resurrection. For example, the power portion of Joseph's story comes not from his palace but his prison years. While being crushed, you're building

Chapter Sixteen

the part of your history that will put power into your testimony."

To sum it up without being extraordinarily spiritual or philosophical, my ministry is all about loving, caring, and sharing. I do not have a title, although if asked what I'd like to be known as, I'd readily say an evangelist. It is not about promoting myself or demanding recognition for being a loving man of God, but of finding infinite worth in EVERY precious life that comes into my care.

I want to be known as the friend who listens without judging and the one who will do all I can to help. I lead people to the Lord and then to a local church, where they can continue to grow in their relationship with God and begin to reach out to others.

The other day, I was introduced by someone as a street evangelist. I loved that! I have always felt that my place is not inside the church, but on the street. Yes, the same streets where those who most need the Lord can be found.

When I think of myself, I cannot help but remember the words I read in one of the books by Ron Hembree: "Jesus seems to delight in lifting the unlikely, the unlovely, and the unwanted." I was one of those, and He in His mercy lifted me to display His glory.

STOP FOR THE ONE

I will never stop my mission to bring glory to His Name. It is my commission, it is my life, it is what I was created to be. I would like to close with the quote by David Cope, from his book, "God's Secret to Greatness:" "When I think of true servants, I often think of the late Mother Teresa, the humble Catholic nun who devoted her life to serving the poor, the destitute and the dying in India's crowded cities. Mother Teresa wouldn't have made it through even one Hollywood screen test. In terms of famous faces or superficially beautiful smiles, she wouldn't have even come close. Yet every leader, celebrity, and power broker on earth wanted to shake her hand or spend time with her. In her final years she barely weighed 70 pounds and her bent frame made it appear as if she were composed mostly of skin and bones. Yet none of these things mattered in the sight of God. He was interested in the way her passion for Christ touched the lives of millions of hurting people over decades of dedicated service to the poorest of the poor to India's 'untouchables.' God was only interested in her heart."

CHAPTER SEVENTEEN

Love as a Way of Life

I am so thankful to the Lord for giving me a ministry that centers on taking the love of Jesus to the streets. I personally believe His heart's desire is to take His Church outside the four walls to meet the broken, hurting, lost, wounded, lonely, forgotten, wandering, and sick ones where they are.

I am glad He did not call me to preach from the pulpit. Not that there is anything wrong with those who speak from there. The Lord did use me in this capacity whenever I was invited to share.

I did so only if the Lord led but I feel my personal calling is more one-on-one, meeting a person individually and introducing them to the love of Christ. If you would ask me what my occupation is, I would say it is to love people.

Tommy Tenney, in his book, "God's Secret to Greatness," said: "God has never been in love with buildings, and He despises anything that separates Him from intimate fellowship with the people He created. He is looking for people who will accept His commission to seek, serve and to save those who are lost.

God wants us to venture beyond the four walls of our worship centers and steepled church buildings to take His light into the darkness and become His hands of mercy and love extended to those who do not know Him."

As I leave my house for the day, my "ministry" is wherever I go. I talk to whomever I come across and try to always bring encouragement or a word of cheer to them. Jesus has filled me with His love, and that love I've received from Jesus is what I love to share with others.

As it says in Matthew 10:8, *"Freely you have received; freely give."*

Talking to strangers has become a way of life for me. I love to start a spontaneous conversation with someone I meet amidst my travels.

There are times when I find a stranger looking very serious. I might ask him, "Is all well? God has given you such a beautiful smile, so why are you so serious?"

Chapter Seventeen

This opens a path for conversation, and we get connected. When we interact with strangers in this way, we will be able to discern why so many are upset and lonely.

I love to take time for people, to make them feel special and cared for. When I see the postman dropping off the mail, I call out to him and thank him for delivering my mail. I inquire about him and his family. At times I invite him in to have a cup of tea. During one such time one of the mailmen became close to me and began to share what was on his heart. As we sat together in my home, I prayed for him and his concerns. I treated him like my own brother—loved and valued. The Lord moved in this postman's heart as he experienced the love of Jesus. He told the other postmen about me, and soon many of them also came to visit.

One Christmas, I invited a group of postmen to my house for a cup of tea with cake and snacks, and shared the love of Jesus with them. I prayed for them and gave each one a copy of the Bible, the New Testament, in their own language. I just delight in loving people with the love of God! I love to care for them. I remember once when the owner of a restaurant started sharing his struggles with me and asked for prayer. We struck up a friendship.

When I would shake hands with him, he would hold the embrace for a long time and not quickly let go. He had been missing out on feeling appreciated in his personal life and was relishing the warmth and love of Jesus through me.

Oh, what great joy when I am able to bring a smile to someone and be His comfort and encouragement! I love to be a carrier of His love, peace, and joy for people. Wherever we go, the fragrance of Jesus should flow from us and draw people to Him.

A ministry such as this requires so little. When I am out in a shop to buy something I need, I speak a compliment to the employee who is assisting me and let them know I appreciate the help. As the barber cuts my hair, we strike up a conversation.

Even as I am just sitting on my scooter at an intersection waiting to go on my way, and I might see another person on a bike, and before we go our different ways, I might ask him his name and admire something he is wearing, or even just tell him that Jesus loves him and is going to grant him the desires of his heart.

For me, there are no strangers, only precious children of the Lord! I make them feel they are important and are noticed.

Chapter Seventeen

To some, I simply tell them that God has a wonderful plan for their life, then bless them on their way.

Whatever the Lord puts in my heart, whether at a crossing on my scooter, or in a shop or a quick stop for something at a random place, I speak the words He has given me for each one.

Not only are we earthly carriers of His divine presence, we should also allow Him to speak words of blessing through us to encourage people in their day. I am sure all of us have received a compliment or other word of encouragement from someone and know how it lifts our spirits!

We are called to boost people out of discouragement. When we look for practical things we can do for others, most times there is great pleasure in doing it. If we do no more than show a little bit of love to people, it can still positively change that person. By sowing a small seed of encouragement into another's life, we also bring joy to the heart of God.

I always spoke to the presser, to whom I would give my clothes for ironing. We would have a casual conversation whenever I visited there, and once I inquired about his little daughter's birthday, whom he had mentioned in a previous discussion.

I bought a dress for his daughter and handed it to him to give it to her. He asked me, "Are you a Father in a church?"

When I asked him why he said that, he replied that he has been around Christians before and they showed such love. He could see love in action through the simple friendship we shared, even though I had never mentioned anything about religion!

This reminds me of the wonderful words of St Francis of Assisi: "Preach always! If necessary, use words." This dear presser soon asked me for a Bible. He wanted to know more about this Jesus and His love!

Does this mean we are called to minister only to unbelievers in this way? No! Once I met a man who was traveling by train to attend a conference in Mumbai.

I struck up a conversation with him and soon realized he was a man of God! Before we reached Mumbai, the Spirit of God told me to bless him with a financial gift. I obeyed and this man was astonished. He shared with me as the tears came that he had decided to obey the Lord and go by faith to attend the conference for 3 days, even staying in a hotel, while fully trusting God for the finances needed! And look how God was lovingly mindful of His children, and so faithful to provide!

Chapter Seventeen

As always, I was only His vessel that was available and FULL of His love so when asked to pour out this blessing, it overflowed to the one I came across.

Heidi Baker, in her book "Learning to Love" says: "It is impossible to be devoted to Jesus and not share Him, pure and simple. We cannot see Him now, but God has ordained that we love Him by loving each other, whom we can see."

I just love to spread His love and joy wherever I go. Many years ago I took a trip to Kashmir. As I went to a travel agent's office to book my return ticket, I started talking with the owner of the agency. We quickly formed a friendship, and he invited me home for a meal. We soon became close friends! What joy was mine to have this opportunity of showing Jesus' love to this precious new friend, with whom I am still in touch. He is Muslim. God loves ALL His children, even those who do not believe in Him, and what an opportunity is ours to just BE His love and spread it to ALL He brings our way.

The question might be, "Do we take time to SHOW His love?" We can become consumed with only speaking about His love and giving a tract, but is it also important not just to share but also show His love through how we live?

STOP FOR THE ONE

I understand that not everyone has the time to strike up a conversation with those they meet all the time. God has given us different ministries and each one's calling is unique to our own spiritual gifts. Giving out tracts with the good news about Jesus has its place.

The Lord can absolutely use that method to speak to a needy heart. And He has done it! However, some of us rely on the same method over and over and expect the same results even when used on different people in different situations.

Methods can be gratifying, but sometimes they don't work because we are called to step out of our comfort zones and BECOME the good news! What if a person has been hurt by a believer?

Do you think they will readily welcome a tract from a stranger about how loving Jesus is? We must remain sensitive to the Spirit's leading and allow Him to show us how to reach a person in the most effective way possible, and never by using a "one-size-fits-all" approach.

Humanity as a whole is touched by a show of genuine concern such as a pat on the shoulder, a loving word, or a listening ear, or even just wanting to know the person's name.

Chapter Seventeen

Later, we can share our testimony and the gift of salvation through Jesus Christ. I have made the habit of writing down their name and later, at home, I pray for them. Even if I only got a few moments to speak with someone in public, you never know what the power of prayer can do as I pray for them at home for as long as I feel led to.

A few moments may be all it takes to make a lasting impression! I have met people and simply asked them if they have anything they need prayer for. Most times if there is a need, that is all it takes for people to open up and share. I go home and lift the person and their burdens to the Lord. Sometimes I find out the outcome of my prayers, other times I do not.

All that matters to me is that I am obedient to the words of Jesus in John 13:34, "*A new commandment I give you: Love one another. As I have loved you, so you also must love one another.*"

Kathy Trocolli from her book, "The Colors of His Love" says: "There are so many needs in the world, it would be easy to be so overwhelmed that you end up doing nothing. But each of us is called to do something. God brings people into our lives and puts them on our minds on a regular basis. We must remain sensitive or we will miss seeing the people God is bringing directly to us. It is these people that we must be generous to, seeking ways to be His love to them."

I remember going to a Catholic bookshop and they had an amazing collection of encouraging bookmarks for sale. I made it a point to buy from there. I used to speak to the nuns who were in the shop and I remember how God brought one nun in particular to share her prayer requests with me. She became a dear sister with whom I became quite close. One year when I rented a hall for the Thanksgiving meeting when my mother shared her testimony, many nuns were in attendance. Isn't it amazing how people from all walks of life and different backgrounds and religions were part of the meeting?

God has given me the grace to love ALL, not seeing religion, caste/social order or background. *"GOD so loved ALL. He gave His only begotten Son, for whosoever believes in Him should not perish but have everlasting life."* [John 3:16]

What does this phrase "God so loved ALL" truly mean? Jesus is not a Christian God, only loving those who put their faith in Him. He is the God of the universe and loves each and every person on the face of the earth. He died for them. He died for you. He died for me. Shouldn't we also love ALL, and BE His love to all, in spite of their background, or religion, or anything else

Chapter Seventeen

that contrasts from us? In spite of differences, we can still LOVE, without compromising our stand.

I remember the time I was admitted to the hospital for four days for a general checkup. The doctor who was attending me was a Hindu. He became a good friend and unknown to me at the time, had been watching how I interacted with others. When I was being discharged, I was taken aback when I noticed this doctor had not put his charges on the bill.

When I thanked him for waiving his charges for the four days that I was admitted, he replied, "You are doing such noble work. It is my joy and privilege to be part of some service to you." My heart was deeply touched by this and I thanked God for him. You may never know who is watching you and the effect your actions with others have on them!

It broke my heart when I read these words by George Sweeting in his book, "Love is the Greatest": "I was shaken by a small newspaper item recently about a fourteen-year-old boy who took his life because 'no one seemed to care.' He had felt no sense of love from anyone except his dog, and in a brief suicide note addressed to his parents he left instructions for the dog's care. NO ONE SEEMED TO CARE. What a stark summation of our world's lack of love—or lack of caring and showing it. Quite likely the boy's parents really did love him, but they evidently failed to let him know it, and his suicide illustrated sharply how minor deeds of lovelessness add up to major tragedies. This boy was searching for love, and he did not find it."

We must never assume who the lonely ones are and who are those who need no encouragement. A perfect example of this is one day when I was driving down the streets of Bangalore.

I saw a traffic police constable at a crossing. The Spirit prompted me to stop and go to him. He looked surprised as I approached. I smiled and asked him his name, then told him he is dear and precious to Jesus, and He loves him. I gave him a bookmark, then drove away. After a few days I saw him at another crossing, and this time he sought me out! He told me he never stopped looking for me every day since the day I went up to him. The words I had spoken and the bookmark I had given him touched his heart and brought great joy and peace to him.

Oh, the love of Christ that penetrates the hearts of people! This constable became very dear to me and we've met quite a number of times since then.

This love of Jesus overflows within our heart until we

Chapter Seventeen

feel we will burst if we do not go share it with others! I am so full of His love that every place I go my eyes keep looking around to reach out and embrace each and every one in Christ.

We must always remember to stay humble and not begin to allow ourselves to feel as though we are a great man or woman of God after we have seen many transformations. We must remember that it is GOD who worked the miracles, not us.

A good example of this is the story of Raju, a young boy who lived in a remote village. He had been attending the prayer meetings at my home and one day asked me to come to his village. He said he would arrange a big meeting and I could preach and share the good news about Jesus with his entire village.

I felt the Spirit of the Lord leading me in a different direction, so I told him I would come to his home with a dear friend who could translate my words from English to Kannada, the local language.

Whoever wanted to attend could come, and I would pray for anyone who had a need. It was a glorious time as so many came for prayer.

There was no preaching, no counseling, no sharing my

testimony—only asking people about their needs, be it physical, emotional, or whatever else, followed by me praying over them.

The Lord began to work, and people were experiencing healing and breakthrough and felt peace like they had never had before. Each time we visited, the numbers of people increased who came for prayer.

Soon we were visiting many homes in the village and seeing even more deliverances! I gave Bibles only to the people who asked for one.

I am very careful to follow the Spirit's leading and take every step slowly and with much prayer, for I do not want to do things according to my own will and plan. God needs to know He can trust His servants when the miracles increase and it becomes easy for His child to feel responsible for the results of his labor. To our Lord belongs all the glory, and we must NEVER feel entitled to share any of it with Him!

It was not me who was a miracle worker who answered prayers, but the Lord. ONLY the Lord. I am a mere vessel, humbled and privileged to serve a great and mighty God.

There have been times I have been taken advantage of

Chapter Seventeen

when someone I ministered to began to take me for granted.

One time a down and out young man who I had found walking along the road shared his story with me about losing a very prestigious job and now could not make ends meet. I invited him and his wife and two children into my home to stay until he could find new employment.

After a while, he got used to being treated like what must have felt like royalty with having a place to stay and all their needs and food provided for, so he began to act very casually about looking for work.

My dear friends who attended the prayer meeting at my home noticed this man was not very serious about trying to find work, and they were very concerned and spoke to me about it.

In her book "The Colours Of His Love," Dee Brestin wrote: "It's no big deal to love the easy ones. Love starts with the hard ones. That's where Jesus comes in."

I could have very easily become frustrated with this man. I began to feel as though I was a guest in HIS home, since he was taking me for granted. I spent much time in prayer over this situation, and God impressed it upon my heart that sometimes He is also in the same situation, where His children take HIM for granted. We get comfortable with His love and goodness and forget to get up and go out and work for Him. How patient and merciful our Lord is towards us!

Armed with this knowledge, I was able to also be patient and merciful with this young family until the day God in His own way provided a way for them to leave and for me to have my home to myself again.

Today, I hear this man and his family are doing well and that he is serving the Lord in another city as an evangelist. They have not had any contact with me since they left, and that is fine. I did what the Lord assigned for me to do for them.

My prayer was then and is now for them to be intimately connected with God and walking in the fear of the Lord while being a testimony of His goodness and grace. That is all that is important.

I love the words of one of my favorite authors, Fawn Parish. In her book "It's All About You, Jesus" she wrote: "Our tenderness towards people must be because God's unfailing love is toward them. We are not responsible for their response to God. We are responsible simply to love. How might Jesus be

Chapter Seventeen

welcomed if we determined to endlessly love the world without regard for response! Someone once said, 'Love them until they ask you why.' That is the best counsel I have heard."

I have struck up conversations with so many people, wherever I go, and am amazed at how God can use such a simple beginning to make a major change in their lives. I have had phone calls from people who found one of the bookmarks I left in a book in the library, saying the verse on the bookmark was exactly the message they needed to hear right at that moment.

It was as if God Himself spoke from His heart to theirs! At times, these phone calls come when I am eating. Without fail, I get up and leave my food to speak to the caller. My mother used to ask why I did not tell the person to call me later since I was having a meal.

I would rather speak to the person then and there and finish the food later, even though it may be cold by the time I get back to it. People and their needs are especially important to me and my food can wait. Food can be re-warmed but I may miss out on ministering to a person for good if I do not attend to them right when they call.

I recall my own experience of the times when I felt down and out. I thought of calling someone and sharing my

STOP FOR THE ONE

heart. It took a bit of courage to make that call but I was desperate for help.

At times I received a cold reply that the person was busy and will get back to me later. Of course, I understand that a person sometimes really is busy, but the tone of his voice was not cordial and compassionate, but almost as if I had bothered them.

At times, "later" was too late.

When I finally received a call back from the person I had wished to speak to, I was no longer in a mind to share my pain. Keeping this in mind, I always try to speak immediately to anyone who calls me, unless of course I am in church, or in a meeting, or in prayer.

My house is always open for people. Yes, people often call me and ask to come at a specific day and time, but I make sure everyone knows there are no appointments necessary if you are in deep pain and need to be attended to immediately. If I already have a visitor and someone else comes for prayer, I welcome the newcomer and lead him into the prayer room. I put on some worship music for him.

The room is surrounded by books and is made to feel comfortable, so I just tell him to feel at home while I

Chapter Seventeen

finish ministering to the other person. I never want anyone to feel unwelcome! It's not a good feeling!

I remember meeting a family in Ooty, a town about 8 hours from my home, and they asked me to visit their home. I did not have their phone number so one evening I simply went to their home and rang the bell.

A man opened the door, looked at me, then said, "Don't you know you need to have an appointment before coming?"

I quietly said that I did not have the phone number, so I could not have called in advance. He gave me the number but did not allow me inside the house.

At this point, my desire to meet with them was gone. I understand it would have been the right thing to call and make an appointment before showing up unannounced, because people have prior commitments. I was at fault. I know this.

Yet couldn't he have allowed me into his house for just 5 minutes and said what he said with love?

All this has taught me to be different and has given me grace to let anyone in real need knock at my door any time of the day or night and be welcomed, for isn't my house truly the Lord's? Again, I am just the steward of

STOP FOR THE ONE

what He has provided for my use to bring others to Him.

I am AVAILABLE 24/7 for Him and for all whom He sends my way. I thank God for ALL the experiences He has allowed me to go through, for they ultimately work for my good. Through these lessons I become a better person, instead of a bitter person.

If only LOVE was not such a rare thing, often missing in the body of Christ! We, who are called to be His hands and His feet sometimes do not want to lift even a finger to help a person in need!

When I visit someone who is in deep pain physically, due to a serious health condition, I do pray for healing, believing God will heal him. But while praying with the person can bring healing, sometimes what is a deeper comfort is to just sit with them as they are in pain, and hold his hand. I make sure he knows he is not alone. He is cared about, and I am there for him, physically. People need our loving care yet sometimes all we do is just pray and leave.

How I remember my own times of deep pain! I longed for a friend who would take time to be with me, but I found none.

My heart ached for the physical presence of someone

Chapter Seventeen

beside me who would help me through my grief, yet I found myself alone.

Even if it means cancelling an appointment, I try very hard to BE THERE for those in pain, for I deeply understand how they are feeling.

No words. No advice, no counseling, or even prayer. Just sitting beside them. There for them, in their time of need.

We have reached the end of the book and I hope your time invested in reading what has been written here has ignited new passion within you, and inspired you to go out and reach others in your own corner of the world with His love.

Our Lord needs you!

I pray that each one of you will experience His unconditional love in new ways, and be FILLED with that love to the point where you cannot help but share what has been given so freely and abundantly to you.

May this account of my experiences spark the desire within you to use the unique gifts our Father has richly blessed you with in new and creative ways. From this day forward, may you make LOVE a way of life!

STOP FOR THE ONE

I would like to challenge you one last time, this time with a quote from Fawn Parish. In her book "It's All About You, Jesus: A Fresh Call to an Undistracted Life." she wrote: "The success of our lives in the end is measured by how well we loved, not how well we produced. When people stand around our grave they are not going to count how many books we wrote, sermons we preached, or companies we founded. They are going to recount that they felt loved by us, that we gave them hope."

ABOUT THE AUTHOR

A man of compassion, Brother Ravi is filled with the love of God, and has been equipped to be emptied into the lives of those who need God's touch.

Where did such a heart come from?

Ravi, who comes from Kolkata (formerly Calcutta), India, and now lives in Bangalore had a staunch Hindu upbringing. When he encountered the love of God through Jesus Christ, his life totally changed forever, as he dedicated himself to being a follower of Jesus.

That decision brought about much persecution from family and others, which led to a radical humbling of his heart as he learned to lean on God, and rely on Him alone in every trying situation that arose. From one who has been through so much, he can readily identify with the suffering of others.

Knowing God has chosen him to reach others has created a deep hunger to deliver God's message to all who will listen, focusing intently on the lost, the lonely, the least, and the last.

The Bible tells us that "faith works by love." The Lord has called Ravi into a life of increasingly extravagant worship and as an intercessory prayer warrior, as he works out his faith through loving God and others.

Brother Ravi has authored another book titled, LOST AND FOUND, which is available on Amazon.

You may contact Brother Ravi at…
gripofgrace309@gmail.com

www.ingramcontent.com/pod-product-compliance
Lightning Source LLC
Chambersburg PA
CBHW072149070526
44585CB00015B/1054